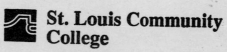

CHARISMATIC CULT LEADERS

CHARISMATIC CULT LEADERS

Thomas Streissguth

The Oliver Press, Inc.
Minneapolis

The Oliver Press, Inc.
Charlotte Square
5707 West 36th Street
Minneapolis, MN 55416-2510

Library of Congress Cataloging-in-Publication Data

Streissguth, Thomas, 1958-
Charismatic cult leaders / Thomas Streissguth.
p.   cm. — (Profiles)
Includes bibliographical references and index.
ISBN: 1-881508-18-8
1. Religious biography—Juvenile literature. [1. Religious leaders.
2. Cults.] I. Title. II. Series: Profiles (Minneapolis, Minn.)
BL72.S77 1995
291'.092'2—dc20
[B]   94-22096
                                                                  CIP
                                                                   AC

ISBN 1-881508-18-8
Profiles XIII
Printed in the United States of America

04 03 02 01 00 99 98   8 7 6 5 4 3 2

Contents

Distinctive clothing, such as that worn by the Hare Krishnas, sometimes serves as a unifying symbol for people with similar religious beliefs.

Introduction

On a wind-swept hill in Texas, a young preacher named David Koresh builds a stockpile of deadly weapons in an isolated compound. More than 100 people join him, convinced the end of the world is coming. After the group's 51-day standoff with federal agents, the compound catches on fire and many inside are burned alive.

In a South American jungle clearing, 914 bodies lie motionless under the tropical sun. These people had lived and worshiped together peacefully until the angry words of their preacher, Jim Jones, persuaded them to drink deadly poison.

Religious faith moved these people to place their lives in the hands of someone else. The belief in gods and supernatural powers is as old as humanity. Some people use religion as a guide to doing good deeds. Others turn to their faith for inspiration or consolation in difficult times. People often rely on religious leaders to help them understand and obey their faith.

Winning the trust of followers requires a very rare human quality called *charisma*. One definition of charisma is the ability to heal the sick and perform other miracles, as Jesus Christ does in the New Testament of the Bible. But charisma also means the ability to influence and control others. Many people seek direction in their lives, answers to their problems, and a leader to guide them. Charismatic leaders use their knowledge and self-confidence to win the trust of these people who are searching for guidance.

People are often manipulated by dynamic religious leaders. Religious groups can turn dangerous when their leaders make themselves the center of their faith and insist on strict and unquestioning obedience. When this type of coercion and control is involved, these groups may be considered *cults*.

Although most religious leaders do not try to exploit their congregations, some people, like Jim Jones and David Koresh, have used holy books and religious doctrines to glorify themselves and gain power. They put themselves above their own faith and lose the direction that religion had once given them. Other religious groups, however, pose little harm to their followers but are perceived as cults because their values are new and differ from those of the larger community. They only become violent when they feel compelled to fight off attacks from outsiders.

Although not everyone agrees on the exact definition of cult, the term usually describes a group of people whose founder is still alive, who may isolate themselves from the outside world, and whose beliefs are considered strange or threatening to outsiders. Some experts estimate that there are at least 500 cults in the United States and 3,000 cults worldwide. According to some estimates, as many as 200,000 people in the United States and 3 million people across the globe belong to cults.

Some of the stories in this book are tragedies, but others are not. Despite their controversial beginnings, some of the religious groups described here have become mainstream churches or survived over the years by splintering into new groups. Others have met with terrible, violent ends. The stories of the charismatic leaders of these groups offer many surprises into the strange and mysterious workings of faith.

Anabaptist leader Jan Beukels (1509-1536)—later known as John of Leiden—led his followers to their deaths while protesting the authority of the Roman Catholic Church.

1

John of Leiden
The Anabaptists of Münster

*T*hroughout most of the Middle Ages, only one church existed in Western Europe—the Roman Catholic Church. Beginning around the twelfth century, the Catholic pope held absolute power over the church and its doctrines. Whoever was pope also controlled church lands and properties across the continent, as well as a huge treasury of gold and precious jewels. Many kings feared the anger of the pope who, they believed, could determine whether someone would spend the afterlife in heaven or hell.

Most people had no way of opposing the church. They obeyed its rules and lived under its protection. During a baptism ceremony, priests would sprinkle water on a newborn's head to welcome the infant into the church. Roman Catholics believed that only people who were baptized would enter heaven after they died. The church used imprisonment, torture, and public execution to punish those who criticized the practice of baptism. Catholic priests followed traditional ceremonies, which were written in ancient Latin, for weddings, festivals, and funerals. But few people other than priests spoke or understood Latin.

In the early sixteenth century, some Christian leaders began to protest the absolute power of the Catholic Church. Some of these "Protestants" believed the church should stop baptizing infants and instead baptize only adults acting of their own free will. As adults, these believers baptized themselves a second time, making a personal decision to join the church. The act of rebaptizing adults who had already been baptized as infants earned this group the name "Anabaptists," meaning those baptized again.

The Anabaptists set themselves apart from society. Living as a community of believers, they shared all of their valuables and held no private property. They rebaptized their followers in private homes, far from any church or Catholic priest. These separatists angered many Protestant leaders, including Martin Luther.

German priest Martin Luther (1483-1546), whose followers are now called Lutherans, was excommunicated from the Roman Catholic Church in 1521 because he tried to change some of the church doctrines and make the scriptures accessible to ordinary citizens.

The Anabaptists also faced a powerful enemy in Charles V, the Holy Roman Emperor who ruled central Europe and was an ally of the Catholic Church. The emperor and the pope condemned Anabaptists as violent, immoral, and dangerous. In 1527, Charles V ordered his soldiers to capture all Anabaptists and put them to death. Over the next few years, the emperor's soldiers hunted down the Anabaptists like wild beasts. After being captured, the Anabaptists were hanged, drowned, beheaded, or burned at the stake. Those who survived the hunt lived in caves and forests, coming out only at night to gather food. Despite these persecutions, the Anabaptists survived, and many peasants and poor laborers joined the movement.

In the early 1500s, Anabaptists were protesting against Catholic control in Switzerland and the Netherlands. But the most famous of these protests took place during several months in the 1530s, when the German town of Münster became a revolutionary Anabaptist kingdom.

Soon after its founding around the year A.D. 800, Münster was ruled by Catholic bishops, who lived outside the town walls. Many townspeople resented the bishops' wealth and power, however. By the 1520s, several

This illustration shows a Roman Catholic church in Europe during the Middle Ages, a time when many people feared to question church authorities.

competing factions fought for control of the town, which then had about 15,000 citizens. Some of the representatives on Münster's 24-member town council remained loyal to the bishop, some worked for the interest of the local tradesmen (who traded largely with Russia and England), and others allied themselves with the Anabaptists.

In 1531, a priest named Bernhard Rothmann, who followed the teachings of Martin Luther, arrived in St. Moritz, a suburb of Münster. Rothmann gained the support of powerful trade organizations, called *guilds*, which represented goldsmiths, bakers, tailors, and other tradesmen. The Catholic bishop of Münster viewed Rothmann as a dangerous rival, but the townspeople liked the Protestant leader's sermons, and he continued preaching.

After the bishop died in May, distrust of Catholics intensified in Münster. Swayed by Rothmann's powerful anti-Catholic sermons, the people of Münster drove out all the Catholic priests and replaced them with Protestants. The new church leaders conducted their services in German instead of Latin, and some Catholics converted and became Anabaptists.

The events in Münster greatly angered Franz von Waldeck, the town's new Catholic bishop. When he demanded that the Protestant priests surrender to the Catholic authorities, the people of Münster prepared for battle. In December 1532, approximately 1,000 residents of Münster marched out of the town and stoned the bishop's palace. They captured many of the bishop's aides and brought their prisoners back to Münster as hostages. Without enough soldiers to rescue his aides or take back the town, the bishop accepted a truce with the town council. He agreed to allow Protestants to preach in the churches and let Münster become a Protestant town.

When they heard about the Protestant victory, thousands of Anabaptists streamed into Münster from the surrounding countryside. Among the new arrivals were Jan Mathys, a baker from the Dutch town of Haarlem, who spoke for the violent overthrow of Catholic priests and bishops. Another immigrant was Jan Beukels, a tailor from the town of Leiden in southern Holland. Paying homage to Jerusalem, which is described as a holy city in the Bible, the two men called Münster the "New Jerusalem." They hoped it would become a place where Anabaptists could live together according to their interpretation of the Bible.

Jan Beukels—who centuries later would be known as John of Leiden—had already traveled widely. He had failed as a businessman, but he was a charismatic speaker and well known to the Dutch Protestants. He loved theatrical effects and had spent much of his time writing and producing his own plays. Although Jan Mathys was not officially a religious leader, he rebaptized Beukels in 1533. Soon after Beukels arrived in Münster in 1534, Mathys and Beukels became the leaders of their own Anabaptist congregation in the town.

In the meantime, Bishop von Waldeck called on Catholic leaders in nearby cities for help and began gathering an army near Münster. The Catholics surrounded the town walls and cut off all supplies of food and arms. Despite the treaty he had signed, the bishop prepared to storm the town and vowed to put all the Anabaptists to death.

Inside Münster's walls, Mathys announced the formation of an exclusively Anabaptist community. By the middle of February 1534, he asked members to give up most of their food, money, and private possessions, which would become the property of the entire town. People ate in communal kitchens, where Anabaptist preachers read from the Bible during meals.

By the end of the month, Mathys announced that everyone still in Münster must convert to Anabaptism. Those who resisted had one week to leave the town or face execution. Fearful for their lives, thousands of Catholics and followers of Martin Luther fled Münster, leaving their possessions and sometimes even their families behind. This was the beginning of a period that would later be called the "Reign of Terror."

Anabaptist men and boys took up arms and prepared to defend the town from the bishop's forces. But five weeks later, Mathys was killed by Catholics while leading a raid with 30 soldiers outside the town walls. Jan Beukels then seized the town and appointed himself "King of Israel." (In the Bible, Israel is the name of the

Münster became one of the key sites of the Anabaptist movement during the sixteenth century, when Jan Beukels was viewed as a dangerous dissenter from the Roman Catholic Church.

kingdom of God's chosen people.) Beukels chose Anabaptist follower Bernhard Knipperdollinck as his second in command. Beukels dissolved the Münster town council and appointed 12 men as "elders of the 12 tribes of Israel." This council would help him control the lives of his followers. Beukels's goal was to establish an exclusively Anabaptist community.

Beukels claimed to receive revelations and instructions directly from God and put into effect a new code of behavior for the citizens of Münster. He burned all letters and books—except for the Bible—and outlawed gambling and drunkenness. Beukels also ordered all adults in Münster to get married, then introduced *polygamy* into the community by declaring that men could have as many wives as they wished. (Every unmarried woman had to marry the first man who proposed to her.) Following this pronouncement, Bernhard Rothmann spoke in the public squares in support of Beukels's policy and chose several wives for himself.

On July 29, Henry Mollenhecke, a resident of Münster who opposed these changes, gathered a crowd of Beukels's opponents and captured Beukels. Mollenhecke threatened to surrender the town to the forces of Bishop von Waldeck if Beukels would not change his ways. After freeing their leader, Beukels's supporters tortured and killed Mollenhecke and about 50 other opponents of polygamy. No one else in Münster dared to oppose their self-proclaimed king.

On August 31, 1534, the bishop's forces stormed the town. Beukels ordered his followers to position themselves along the edge of the town wall. The people of Münster held their fire until the Catholic army was at the foot of the town wall. Then they attacked the besiegers with cannon balls, arrows, and rocks. The bishop's forces retreated in panic, and von Waldeck decided to enforce a strict blockade of Münster rather than risk the lives of any more soldiers in futile assaults.

Beukels celebrated this victory by having himself crowned in a town square as the "King of Righteousness." Wearing a robe of royal purple, he appeared three times each week in the marketplace, where the citizens of Münster gave him a special throne. The people of the town prostrated themselves on the ground before him and, in return for this worship, Beukels provided feasts and entertainments for his subjects. At one of these outdoor festivals, Beukels and one of his "queens" posed as servants and served food and wine to the townspeople.

The bishop's blockade, nevertheless, was preventing food from entering the town. During the autumn and winter, hunger gradually overtook Münster. After the people had eaten all of their livestock, they were forced to eat their dogs and cats. Later, they captured frogs and rats and gathered grass and moss. Finally, they ate the leather of their own shoes. The people of Münster were starving to death. By spring, the population had fallen from thousands to a few hundred. Beukels no longer had enough guards to post at all of the town gates or defend the entire town wall.

In May, a resident of Münster who had grown disloyal to the Anabaptists left the town and told the Catholic authorities which gates around the town were undefended. On June 25, 1535, the bishop ordered an attack. Several hundred well-armed horsemen and foot soldiers forced their way into the town. A fierce battle took place in Münster's streets and houses. Many officials

20

of the town, including priest Bernhard Rothmann, were killed.

As the defenders lost ground, the bishop's troops gradually forced the Anabaptists into the central marketplace, where Beukels prepared for a last stand. Fearing a further loss of his own troops, the bishop asked Beukels if he would be willing to call a truce. If the Anabaptists would lay down their arms and surrender, the bishop would spare their lives.

The leaders of Münster agreed to the truce. But shortly after the fighting stopped, the bishop's troops began another bloody massacre that lasted for two days. They hunted down Anabaptists and killed them in their homes. The only Anabaptists who left the town alive were Jan Beukels and a few of his aides, whom the bishop took as prisoners. He was determined to make a terrifying example of Beukels. For six months, the Catholics paraded Beukels through the surrounding countryside.

On January 22, 1536, the bishop ordered his soldiers to execute the Anabaptist leader. Soldiers tied Beukels to a stake and bound him with an iron collar. They poked at his body with white-hot tongs until they could smell his burned flesh. Then they stuck the tongs in his mouth and tore out his tongue. The horror continued as one soldier drove a dagger through Beukels's heart. Finally, the executioners stuffed his body and those of two other Münster rebels into iron cages and hung them from the towers of the Church of St. Lambert.

The Anabaptist revolt was over. For centuries afterward, the Holy Roman Emperor and other European rulers banned the very word *Anabaptist* in parts of Europe. Catholic officials used the siege of Münster as a stern warning to others to adhere to the teachings of the Catholic Church. Although the church captured and executed thousands of Anabaptists, the sect survived in various forms after the fall of Münster.

The followers of Menno Simons, a former Catholic priest from Holland who became an important Anabaptist leader, carried on their doctrines in northern Europe and Russia. Known as "Mennonites," these Anabaptists escaped persecution by fleeing eastward to the Ukraine or

Dutch priest Menno Simons (1496?-1561) left the Roman Catholic Church in 1536 because he no longer believed in infant baptism and other practices supported by the church.

heading across the Atlantic Ocean. The first Mennonite settlement in North America was formed in 1683 in Germantown, Pennsylvania. They later established independent communities in Kansas, Nebraska, and other parts of the Midwest.

In the nineteenth century, Jacob Ammann, a Swiss Mennonite leader, founded a group that believed in separating themselves completely from people of other faiths. His followers, called the Amish, arrived in North America in 1728. They settled in several states, including Ohio, Pennsylvania, Indiana, Iowa, Illinois, and Wisconsin. Today, the Amish still live in separate communities and remain apart from the modern world. They seldom use electricity, telephones, or cars. Horse-drawn carriages usually serve as their transportation, and the Amish grow their own food and make much of their own clothing.

Today, few people know about Anabaptism's violent beginnings. They have never heard of Jan Beukels from the town of Leiden and the siege of Münster. Nevertheless, many of the doctrines first preached by Beukels more than 450 years ago have survived in the beliefs of the Amish and Mennonites.

Although many people were hostile toward Mormon prophet Joseph Smith (1805-1844) during the nineteenth century, most people now consider Mormonism a mainstream religion.

2

Joseph Smith
The Church of Jesus Christ
of Latter-day Saints

*D*uring the early 1800s, many new religious sects were growing in the United States. In eastern cities and on the distant frontier, dozens of religious denominations tried to spread their unique set of beliefs to farmers, townspeople, and pioneers. But not everyone was tolerant of other religions. Some groups, such as the Quakers, were physically beaten because of their beliefs. Others, including Roman Catholics, were sometimes outlawed from holding public office.

In these uncertain times, some people, like the Smiths of Palmyra, New York, weren't sure what to believe. Lucy Smith and her husband, Joseph Sr., spent many hours reading the Bible. Lucy had been raised Presbyterian, but Joseph Sr., who claimed that he sometimes received visions from heaven, did not put his faith in any organized church.

One of the Smiths' sons, Joseph Jr., said that he, too, sometimes heard voices and had mysterious visions. The first vision occurred in the spring of 1820, when he was 14 years old. While he was exploring the woods near the family farm, a shaft of bright light descended from the sky, and two messengers from heaven appeared. These angels told young Joseph that he must not join any church.

Three years later, Joseph had another vision. One night, an angel named Moroni appeared in Joseph's room, telling him that a set of golden tablets and a pair of magic stones were buried on the nearby hill of Cumorah. According to the angel, Joseph could use these "seeing stones" to translate the inscriptions on the tablets.

The following day, Joseph said, he walked the three miles to the hill of Cumorah, where he dug up a small box. Inside the box, he found a set of stones and thin, metallic sheets about eight inches square and covered with strange symbols. When Joseph tried to remove the "golden plates," an angel appeared, warning him that the box was not to be disturbed or removed.

Joseph Smith had to wait four years—until 1827—before the angel allowed him to take the box, the plates, and the seeing stones home to his family. Local Protestants believed that miraculous events, like those Joseph described, had ended during biblical times, but several neighbors and friends still came to the farm to see the mysterious buried treasure. Joseph was very protective of the plates and refused to show them to other people, though a few people later claimed that they, too, had seen the plates.

To get away from his skeptical neighbors, Joseph Smith moved to Harmony, Pennsylvania, later in 1827. There, he proposed to translate the golden plates with the help of Martin Harris, a farmer, and Oliver Cowdery, a teacher from Palmyra. In the days that followed, Joseph sat behind a curtain to hide the plates from view. Using the seeing stones to translate, he read the inscriptions out loud while Harris or Cowdery wrote down what they heard. After several weeks, he finished the translation, which he called The Book of Mormon. The book was more than 500 pages long, and the first 5,000 copies were printed in March 1830. By this time, Joseph Smith had married a woman from Pennsylvania named Emma Hale, who encouraged her husband's religious endeavors.

In the next month, Joseph Smith and Oliver Cowdery baptized each other in the nearby Susquehanna River. They became the first "elders," or leaders, of

Joseph Smith's new church. They believed that people should be baptized only when they were old enough to understand the meaning of the ceremony and that the Book of Mormon should be used as a companion to the Bible.

The Book of Mormon told an amazing tale about a prophet named Lehi, who had sailed to North America

This illustration shows the angel of John the Baptist— Jesus Christ's cousin, according to the Bible—ordaining Joseph Smith and Oliver Cowdery as priests.

from Palestine around 600 B.C. According to the book, Lehi's sons, Laman and Nephi, became bitter rivals and each formed a powerful army. Centuries later, while their followers—the Lamanites and the Nephites—prepared for battle in the area that would become the state of New York, a Nephite named Mormon recorded the story of the battle and earlier events on a set of golden tablets. The Lamanites slaughtered many of the Nephites, but Mormon's son, Moroni, survived and buried the tablets at Cumorah. Nearly 1,500 years later, Joseph Smith claimed that the angel of Moroni had appeared to him.

Joseph Smith encountered many disbelievers. Several eastern newspapers mocked The Book of Mormon, and preachers from New York City to Boston called Smith a fraud. Smith countered by insisting that he was only restoring Christianity to its original doctrines, as had been revealed to him through his visions. Despite his critics, some people—especially those who did not belong to an already established church—believed in Joseph Smith's message.

The first members of the Mormon Church eagerly spread the word of Smith's visions and divine revelations. They claimed that their leader was a prophet who could hear the voice of God. Smith's own sermons converted numerous people in western New York. A tall man with a strong and forceful way of speaking, Joseph Smith convinced many listeners of the truth of his claims. Smith soon had 70 dedicated followers, including his older brother, Hyrum.

To expand the church's membership, Smith sent missionaries to New England, and Oliver Cowdery spread the Mormon gospel as far west as the Missouri frontier. But Smith's greatest success came in the town of Kirtland, Ohio, where a preacher named Sidney Rigdon had founded a small religious community. Inspired by Joseph Smith's preaching, Rigdon became a convert to Mormonism, and many residents of Kirtland also joined the Mormon Church.

The criticism and condemnation he faced in New York prompted Smith to move to Kirtland in 1831. There, he ordained all male Mormons as priests in his church, giving them the religious authority to hold services and proclaim the gospel of The Book of Mormon. Kirtland soon became a Mormon community where the believers attempted to share all private property in common. Mormon families turned their crops over to the church, which then supplied each family with the food it needed.

Despite Smith's popularity, many people still doubted his claims. Threatened by these skeptics, Smith had a dream of an ideal city of God, where he could build a church free from the pressures and dangers of the eastern United States. He called the city "New Jerusalem," paying homage to the city of Jerusalem, which is mentioned frequently in the Bible. New Jerusalem would be a place of refuge, where people could live under their leader's guidance.

When Oliver Cowdery and other missionaries returned from Missouri, they said they had found a perfect location for New Jerusalem: a frontier town called Independence, which is located on the Missouri River, near Kansas City. After hearing these reports, Smith had another revelation. This time, he was told to move the Mormons west. Late in the summer of 1831, a wagon train, led by Sidney Rigdon and Joseph Smith, started out from Ohio and began rolling across the Midwest.

Soon after reaching Independence, Missouri, however, the Mormons experienced problems. The land was poor for home sites, and few of them knew how to farm. Many of the Mormon settlers were also plagued by loneliness and uncertainty. That autumn, Rigdon and Smith decided to return to Kirtland, leaving the Mormon pioneers behind in Missouri.

The settlement struggled in Missouri, but the followers of Joseph Smith aroused the anger of other nearby settlers, many of whom believed that the Mormons had made an alliance with the Indians to steal their land. Many non-Mormon settlers were also upset with the Mormons' anti-slavery views, since slaves still worked many Missouri farms and plantations.

A violent rebellion against the Mormons began brewing in 1832. When Smith and Rigdon returned to Independence to calm the situation, a group of non-Mormons captured them, tied them up with ropes, and dragged them for miles across the hard, stony ground before releasing them. Through the summer and autumn of 1833, local residents tore down Mormon cabins, destroyed a printer's shop that had published Smith's revelations, and drove Mormon settlers from their homesteads.

When the Mormons asked the state government for help, the governor of Missouri and leaders of the state militia refused to lend any assistance because they saw the Mormons as troublemakers who would be better off living somewhere else. To defend their church, the Mormons back in Kirtland organized a militia of their own, arming more than 200 men with muskets, pistols, and swords, and prepared to travel to Missouri.

In Missouri, wild rumors began spreading about an incoming Mormon invasion, and many Missouri settlers believed that the Mormons intended to drive them out of Missouri and establish an independent government dedicated to the teachings of Joseph Smith. As the Mormon army drew near, local authorities and Missouri Governor Daniel Dunklin threatened to call out their militias and meet force with force.

Because the long march from Ohio brought sickness and hunger to the Mormon army, the forces weakened, and Smith decided to offer a peace plan. He said he would buy out the property of all those opposed to the Mormon settlement, subtracting the cost of damage already done to Mormon property. When his opponents turned down this proposal, Smith decided to return to Ohio with his army, rather than face Missouri's strong militia.

Back in Kirtland, Smith spent three years building his church—now officially known as the Church of Jesus Christ of Latter-day Saints—with the help of visions he received. According to one of these visions, Mormons would no longer be required to turn over all their crops to the church. Instead, they could keep what they needed for survival and only turn over any surplus.

At the same time, the church was going through a financial crisis. Smith and his followers had borrowed thousands of dollars to buy new land, but the value of land was falling and many of Kirtland's businesses closed. The crisis emptied the church treasury and threatened to leave the Mormon leaders penniless. Martin Harris and Oliver Cowdery turned against their prophet, and other angry followers denounced Smith as well. On the night of January 12, 1838, one of the former Mormons swore out a warrant for Smith's arrest on charges of fraud.

Smith fled Ohio and traveled to Far West, a new Missouri settlement that had been built by Mormons from Independence. Although the city had thrived at first, it was now suffering hard times at the hands of enemies who stole the Mormons' cattle, burned their fields, and threatened to drive them out of the state. To defend Far West and other Mormon settlements, Smith and his aides organized the "Armies of Israel," an allusion to the nation of Israel, which the Bible describes as holy.

The situation grew tense and soon led to open warfare. In the summer of 1838, Mormons and Missourians fought with knives and rifles in the fields and forests of western Missouri. In late October, after a company of 60 Mormon soldiers defeated a Missouri militia, Governor Lillburn Boggs ordered a counterattack. The state militia massacred 17 Mormon settlers in a blacksmith's shop at the settlement of Haun's Mill.

Realizing that his forces were overpowered, Smith decided to ask the state for peace. General Samuel Lucas, the leader of the Missouri militia, demanded that Smith surrender and turn over all Mormon property. But immediately after Smith and four of his followers had given themselves up, Lucas ordered them to be shot the following day without standing trial.

Lucas put Smith in the custody of a militia company under General Alexander Doniphan. But Doniphan decided that he could not shoot the Mormons without a trial, so he left his prisoners in the custody of General Lucas. Lucas brought Smith to Independence for a hearing, where several Mormons testified against their leader. (Lucas had arrested 40 Mormons who had intended to defend their leader in court.) After listening to the one-sided testimony, Judge Austin King, who disapproved of the Mormons' beliefs, ordered Smith arrested and held in jail for treason.

Brigham Young, one of Smith's loyal aides, gathered food for the Missouri Mormons and prepared to escape with them to Illinois. Through the winter of 1838-1839, Young brought food and other supplies to Smith's followers and led the Mormons eastward across the Mississippi River.

In April 1839, Smith's captors moved him to another county to stand trial. Anti-Mormon sentiment ran high there, however. Fearing that the state could not find enough impartial jurors to give Smith a fair trial, the

Mormon leader Brigham Young (1801-1877) sometimes led the Church of Jesus Christ of Latter-day Saints in Joseph Smith's absence.

judge ordered a change of the trial site and arranged an escort for Smith. While being brought to the new location, Smith escaped.

After his escape, Joseph Smith found a promising site for a new settlement on a wooded hill along the east bank of the Mississippi River in Illinois. Within a year, his followers had built 250 houses in the new Mormon city of Nauvoo, whose name was derived from the Hebrew words for "city" and "beautiful." The town prospered as newcomers arrived from New England and Europe, bringing enough money for new investments. Nauvoo soon became one of the largest cities on the frontier.

Joseph Smith became mayor and the head of the city council, which had the power to accept or reject licenses for new businesses. He also controlled the buying and selling of land and homes. To celebrate their peace

36

and prosperity, the Mormons built a magnificent new temple on the highest point of the riverbank.

Having escaped Missouri as a fugitive, Smith was now determined to make the Church of Jesus Christ of Latter-day Saints a powerful force—one that the state of Illinois and its people would never dare to attack. To defend the city, he formed the Nauvoo Legion, which drafted every able-bodied man between the ages of 18 and 45. The Legion would also protect Smith from the raids of sheriffs, who were still determined to bring him back to Missouri for trial.

This illustration shows the Nauvoo Temple, which was located in the Illinois town Joseph Smith called "city beautiful."

Although the people of Illinois prided themselves on their tolerance of others, many of them grew to dislike the Mormons and suspected Smith and his aides of blasphemy and false prophecy. Non-Mormons also feared the forces of the Nauvoo Legion. Furthermore, many Illinois legislators suspected that Smith had plans to set up a Mormon nation, which would be independent of the U.S. government. Strange rumors were also spreading about the marriage practices of Smith's followers in Nauvoo.

Joseph Smith, in fact, had begun teaching a secret doctrine modeled after the Old Testament figure of Jacob, who had two wives and whose sons and grandsons were the founders of the 12 tribes of Israel. According to Smith, Mormon leaders—all of whom were men—could follow the example of Jacob and take more than one wife.

In the early 1840s, Smith began performing secret marriage ceremonies for himself and his new wives in the Nauvoo temple. Many of these new brides were already married to other men. Smith himself eventually had more than 20 wives, and several of them were already married.

Many of Smith's aides in the church eagerly adopted this new doctrine, but problems arose when the men fought over their new spouses. Both Smith and John Bennett, a recent convert to Mormonism, wanted to marry Nancy Rigdon, the daughter of Sidney Rigdon. To get rid of his rival, Smith threw Bennett out of the Mormon Church.

38

In 1842, Bennett publicly accused the Mormons of practicing *polygamy*—having more than one wife at a time—and Joseph Smith of setting up a dictatorship in Nauvoo. According to Bennett, Smith planned to become the monarch of an independent empire. Bennett also insisted that the Mormon leader had appointed 12 of his most trusted aides—whom the angry ex-Mormon called the Destroying Angels—to track down and kill enemies of the church.

Furthermore, Bennett accused Smith of paying an assassin to kill Governor Boggs of Missouri, who had been shot and wounded by an unknown assailant in 1842. After recovering from his injuries, the governor ordered Missouri officers to ride to Nauvoo and arrest Smith. When they arrived, however, the Mormon courts in Nauvoo stopped the arrest order. Thomas Ford, the governor of Illinois, agreed to hear Joseph Smith's arguments in court. With a heavily armed escort, Smith rode into Springfield, the state capital, where the court decided in favor of the Mormons and said Bennett had been lying.

Determined to protect himself further, Smith established an independent government in Nauvoo and, in December 1843, asked the U.S. Congress for permission to create an independent territory. Instead of separating church and state, as the U.S. Constitution demands, Joseph Smith used religious doctrines to create and enforce laws.

Anti-Mormon hostility intensified when Smith announced his plans to create a new political party and run for the U.S. presidency. Newspaper editors and public officials feared that a union of church and state under Joseph Smith (who wanted a "man of God" in office) would become a *theocracy*—a government of religious leaders.

By now, the practice of polygamy among the Mormon leaders was well known to the town's residents, and editorials in the Nauvoo *Expositor* newspaper attacked Smith for his multiple marriages and for his presidential ambitions. When the people of Nauvoo read about these multiple marriages, some of them turned against their leader.

The Nauvoo city council found the *Expositor* guilty under the town's "public nuisance" law and ordered its destruction. A mob loyal to Smith attacked the newspaper offices, burning copies of the *Expositor* and destroying the *Expositor* printing press. Following this attack, other Illinois newspapers printed false stories of rampaging Mormon armies and of Joseph Smith's orders to pillage and burn down the homes of non-Mormons. After reading these accounts, Governor Ford ordered Joseph Smith to give himself up for trial in Carthage, an Illinois town about ten miles from Nauvoo. Smith and a small group of his followers were charged with polygamy, arson, and treason, and Ford set out for Nauvoo with a company of militia to apprehend the Mormon leader.

Fearing an attack by his enemies, Smith asked for an armed escort out of Nauvoo—but Ford refused. When Joseph Smith slipped across the Mississippi River with his brother Hyrum, the Mormons of Nauvoo became terrified. They felt helpless without their leader. A plea from Joseph's first wife, Emma Hale Smith, convinced the two brothers to return to Nauvoo and to give themselves up to the Illinois authorities.

On June 24, 1844, Joseph, Hyrum, and a small group of followers left for Carthage, where local militiamen greeted them with insults and threw them into jail. The guards uttered promises to kill their Mormon prisoners at the earliest opportunity. Still interested in reaching a peaceful settlement, Governor Ford decided to journey to Nauvoo and address the Mormons there. Smith pleaded to go with the Illinois governor, but Ford refused to take Smith with him.

When Ford left Carthage on the morning of June 27, there was no one left in town to protect the rights of Smith and his followers. A mob of more than 200 people—including some militia members—surrounded the jail. Angry men ran inside to attack the Mormons while members of the crowd shot at the jail. Joseph Smith fell to the ground while trying to escape from his upstairs jail cell, and a gun shot from point-blank range ended his life.

The death of Joseph Smith did not bring about the downfall of the church he had founded. Instead, his followers left Illinois and rode the wagon trails that reached the western frontier. Led by Brigham Young, the Mormons arrived in the Great Basin of the Rocky Mountains, where they founded Salt Lake City in 1847.

The U.S. government would not allow the Mormons to establish an independent state in the desert—especially since many Mormons were still practicing polygamy. In 1857, a brief conflict erupted between the Mormons and U.S. troops. In 1890, the Mormons gave up polygamy and agreed to abide by U.S. laws and the Constitution. The federal government admitted their territory to the Union as the state of Utah in 1896.

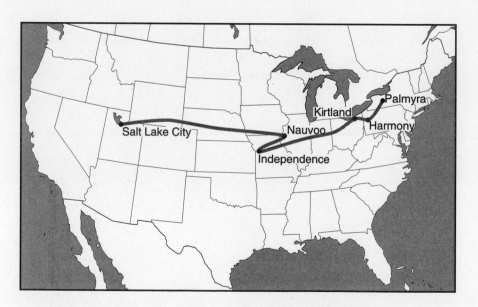

The early Mormons—who faced hostility in Palmyra, Harmony, Kirtland, Independence, and Nauvoo—did not receive general acceptance until reaching Salt Lake City.

Over the past 100 years, Mormon missionaries have continued to found new settlements and travel throughout the world to gain converts. Nearly 9 million people now call themselves Mormons, and the church owns colleges, seminaries, and church-affiliated businesses worldwide. The Mormons have thrived largely because the leaders of the church adapted their sect to some of the demands of the outside world. Despite these changes, the teachings of Joseph Smith still form the basis of Mormon beliefs.

A monument to Joseph Smith stands in Salt Lake City, the final home of the Church of Jesus Christ of Latter-day Saints.

George Baker Jr. (1877?-1965), better known as Father Divine, called his followers "angels"—and some of them believed he was God.

3

Father Divine
The Peace Mission

The day is half over in the quiet town of Sayville, New York. Inside the house at 72 Macon Street, several dozen people sing and talk around a large banquet table. Newcomers walking in from the street see a neatly dressed gentleman at the head of the table. With a serene and patient expression, he raises his hand for silence.

All eyes are upon Father Divine as he welcomes the new members to the banquet and says a few words of dedication. Then, the women working in the kitchen help him to begin serving the plentiful dinner. There are sweet potatoes, squash, and cucumbers. Pasta and rice dishes also make the rounds, as well as platters of chicken, ham, and roast beef. Afterward, several flavors of ice cream arrive for dessert. In the middle of the table, a never-ending fountain of fresh milk flows from a spigot. While they eat, the diners murmur their heartfelt thanks to the man at the head of the table. The newcomers have never seen such an abundance of food, nor have they ever experienced such kindness and fellowship.

The banquet is taking place in the early 1930s, in the middle of the Great Depression. During a time when one out of four workers is unemployed and millions of families are going hungry, Father Divine and his devoted follow-ers—called "angels"—provide a seemingly endless supply of free food and good will. As the diners complete their feast and rise, more people wait in the living room to take their place at the banquet table. By the end of the day, hundreds of people will have been fed.

Father Divine told his grateful followers very little about his past. Many of them didn't know that his real name was George Baker Jr. or that he was from Savannah, Georgia. Born sometime between 1877 and 1883 to George and Nancy Baker, two former slaves who had won their freedom after the Civil War, George Jr. grew up in a small log cabin in the town of Rockville, Maryland. As a young man, George Jr. left home for the city of Baltimore, where many black migrants from the country-side were seeking a better life.

When George Baker arrived in Baltimore in 1899, he discovered that the city wasn't much of an improvement over what he had known in Rockville. The black people of Baltimore lived in poor ghetto neighborhoods filled with crime, alcoholism, and hunger. Few jobs were available to them, and the wages they earned were barely enough for survival. Like most of his neighbors, Baker began searching for a way out.

Baker soon had the chance to move into the servants' quarters of a large house that belonged to an elderly, white businessman named William Ortwine. Working as a gardener for Ortwine and his neighbors,

George Baker Jr. came to Baltimore in 1899 looking for a better life. Instead, he found people in need of hope.

Baker earned about 50 cents a day—enough to support himself. He also became a regular churchgoer and began to think about becoming a preacher.

At that time, the Christian churches of Baltimore were strictly separated by race. On Sunday mornings, whites and blacks attended their own Methodist, Baptist, and Episcopal churches. Baker avoided "mainstream" black churches and instead went back to the ghetto and preached in small, storefront churches. These storefronts attracted people who didn't like the solemn services of mainstream churches. Many of them were rural migrants who were poor, sick, or down on their luck. Instead of a sermon, they wanted inspiration. Enthusiastic and claiming to be filled with God's Holy Spirit, storefront preachers would sing and shout their lessons to thrill their congregations.

George Baker worked out his own particular brand of religion, which combined elements from various Christian denominations. His study of the Bible led him to believe that God and the Holy Spirit were present in all people. He also believed that if people could find the Holy Spirit within themselves, they would be able to overcome sickness and poverty.

Baker believed people could discover the Holy Spirit through "New Thought," a philosophy that was spreading rapidly in the United States. According to New Thought, positive thinking was the key to wealth and happiness. Anyone seeking prosperity and success had to banish

48

negative thoughts and overcome their fear of failure. He saw New Thought as a way for black people to overcome the obstacles of racism. Instead of seeking consolation for their troubles in a big, organized church, his listeners could use religion to obtain independence and self-respect. What's more, they could drop the traditional Christian notion of life after death and instead find "heaven on earth" while they were still alive.

In 1906, Baker traveled to California, where new religions and New Thought were catching on fast. There, he experienced a sudden and powerful revelation to leave behind his old identity and spread his message of self-help and heaven on earth all over the country. When Baker returned to Baltimore, he organized a small group of followers, and they suggested he begin calling himself the "Messenger."

The Messenger preached in homes, on street corners, and at storefront churches, and people listened to him. He refused all donations from his followers and depended on the hospitality of his friends and converts. He won supporters to his ideas by inviting listeners to his Holy Communion banquets, which were modeled after the biblical description of the Last Supper. Following the example of Jesus Christ during his last meal with his disciples, the Messenger personally blessed the generous helpings of delicious food. He delivered his sermon while his guests and loyal followers ate.

Three "angels" prepare large meals for a Holy Communion banquet.

In 1912, the Messenger journeyed to Georgia and began preaching to small black congregations. Many white people in the area didn't appreciate black people hearing about self-help and positive thinking, however. In 1913, local authorities arrested the Messenger after an argument with ministers in Savannah. He was sentenced to serve 60 days on a chain gang.

After his release, Baker traveled to Valdosta, Georgia. He converted several women in Valdosta who heard the Messenger's sermons and believed that he, like God, was "divine." The Messenger's popularity again got him into serious trouble, however, when he was arrested by a local sheriff and charged with lunacy. Nevertheless, the Messenger didn't stop preaching. From his jail cell, he converted several other inmates. In February 1914, a skilled white attorney helped him beat the charges.

The Messenger immediately left Valdosta and moved to Brooklyn, New York. There, he set up a house that offered food, shelter, and companionship. The members pooled their wages and shared their belongings. By helping his unemployed converts find work, the Messenger showed them a road out of poverty.

In New York, the Messenger also met a woman named Penninah, who suffered from severe rheumatism, which caused her so much pain that she had trouble walking. The couple fell in love and eventually got married. On the wedding certificate, the Messenger changed his name to Reverend Major Jealous Divine. His followers began calling him Father Divine—and sometimes addressed him simply as "God." Penninah, meanwhile, adopted the name Mother Divine.

Father Divine's Holy Communion banquets won him many new converts in New York City. But the metropolis was a noisy and crowded place, where hundreds of churches and thousands of preachers competed for hearts and souls. In the autumn of 1919, Father Divine moved out of New York City and purchased a house in Sayville, a mostly white town on Long Island.

Father Divine called his new house the Refuge Home for the Poor Only. People down on their luck could knock on his door any time of the day; he promised to turn no one away. Guests listened to their host preach about honesty, hard work, and positive thinking. When he asked them to rise from their seats and tell their life stories, they responded with shouts of encouragement. Laughter, singing, and dancing at the Refuge Home went on late into the night. Father Divine's house soon became known as Father Divine's Kingdom. The leader of this realm began building a network of storefront churches and communes in other cities.

Father Divine made additions to his house and bought new, expensive cars that lined the driveway. Dozens—sometimes hundreds—of people arrived every day to enjoy his banquets and sermons. But the gatherings caused noise and commotion, and Divine's white neighbors worried that black people in Sayville would hurt the value of white-owned homes.

On Sunday, November 15, 1931, the local police arrested Father Divine and his followers for "creating a public nuisance," and authorities set a date for a trial. Of the 78 people arrested, 15 were white and 63 were black; 46 pleaded guilty to disturbing the peace and received $5 fines, while the other 32 remained as defendants. By this time, a group of Sayville residents had formed a committee to find some way to get rid of Father Divine. After the preacher's arrest, the committee proposed that the city drop its charges against Divine if he would promise to move out of town. But since the committee had no legal authority, the preacher's trial went ahead.

Although his followers crowded the courtroom, Father Divine found no sympathy from the jurors or from Judge Lewis Smith. Judge Smith, a strict Presbyterian churchgoer, publicly said he believed the defendant was guilty of fraud and blasphemy. On June 5, the jury found Father Divine guilty as charged, and Judge Smith sentenced him to a year in jail and gave him a $500 fine. Four days later, the judge, who had a history of heart disease, died of a heart attack.

Some people claimed that Father Divine had used supernatural powers to get back at Judge Smith, but Father Divine told his followers that negative thoughts were the real cause of Smith's death. Father Divine was released from jail on June 25 after paying $5,000 bail. He appealed his sentence, and the court agreed that the late Judge Smith had been too harsh and gave Father Divine his freedom.

Father Divine's Kingdom grew rapidly as he founded new communal houses, called "Peace Missions," all across the nation. By 1934, more than 100 branches of the Peace Mission existed in the United States. Some of Father Divine's "angels" helped to run the mission homes, which offered shelter and food to the poor and the homeless, with separate dormitories for men and women. A Peace Mission training program helped unemployed people look for work. The missions held Holy Communion banquets regularly, with a place at the head of the table always reserved for Father Divine.

Riding in a Rolls-Royce, Father Divine greets some of his followers in Harlem.

People who came to the missions shared amazing success stories. One poor woman named Viola Wilson was almost dead from hunger when she found refuge in a Peace Mission in New Jersey. She recovered under the care of Father Divine's angels. She named herself Faithful Mary.

Along with his strong religious faith, Father Divine had a sharp head for business. He used the money donated by his followers to establish restaurants, laundries, hotels, and retail stores. Members of the Peace Mission ran the businesses and shared the profits. Because the workers received little or no wages, these businesses could charge very low prices for their goods and services.

With his wealth and power growing, Father Divine looked beyond sermons and religion and began to take an interest in worldly matters. He announced his goal of cleaning up government by getting rid of corrupt politicians. He also proposed new laws against racial segregation and lynching, and he urged his followers to vote for candidates who supported his goals.

In 1936, the Peace Mission purchased dozens of farms, homes, and businesses in upstate New York, where Father Divine started a project called the Promised Land. His followers pooled their labor and resources to raise crops to be shipped to Peace Mission banquets and grocery stores.

Seeing an opportunity to achieve nationwide popularity during the 1936 presidential campaign, Father Divine organized an International Divine Righteous Government Convention. His political platform demanded an end to lynchings and capital punishment, the destruction of all weapons of war, and an end to racism by desegregating schools and passing laws guaranteeing equal rights for everyone. The Peace Mission centers launched voter-registration drives, and Father Divine's followers set up Righteous Government departments to enlist the support of prominent politicians.

The Peace Mission delivered its Righteous Government platform to both the Republicans and the

Democrats during the 1936 national political conventions, but neither political party wanted to risk losing votes by supporting this controversial religious leader. By this time, Father Divine had many enemies who believed he was taking advantage of his followers. Mainstream churches opposed him, and many religious leaders were suspicious of his claims. When he realized that most people outside of the Peace Mission were ignoring the Righteous Government platform, Father Divine asked his followers not to vote in the upcoming election.

Soon afterward, Father Divine found himself at the center of a national scandal. It began in California, where a wealthy Peace Mission member named John Wuest Hunt began holding banquets and placing himself at the unused seat at the head of the table that had been left vacant in honor of Father Divine. Calling himself John the Revelator, Hunt proclaimed himself to be Jesus Christ, the Son of God.

At a Peace Mission meeting in Denver that December, Hunt met a 17-year-old girl named Delight Jewett. Hunt was convinced that Delight was the second coming of the Virgin Mary, whom the New Testament describes as Jesus Christ's mother. Hunt brought Jewett back to California, then announced plans to marry her and have a child, whom they would name the "New Redeemer."

Father Divine denounced Hunt and asked Delight Jewett to move to one of the Peace Mission farms in

*According to the New Testament, the Virgin Mary
gave birth to Jesus Christ, the Son of God.*

upstate New York. Instead, Delight's parents removed her
from the Peace Mission and demanded a settlement in
cash for their trouble. When Father Divine refused, the
Jewetts sold their story to the *New York Evening Journal*,
and the newspaper alerted the Federal Bureau of
Investigation. While fascinated readers bought up copies
of the *Journal*, a nationwide police hunt for John the
Revelator was underway.

Eventually, Hunt gave himself up to the FBI, but
that didn't stop more stories about the Peace Mission
from hitting the press. Several former members accused

Father Divine of stealing their money and belongings. They also claimed he had forced his followers to work like slaves in the Peace Mission homes and businesses.

Even after a federal court in Los Angeles found John the Revelator guilty of kidnapping Delight Jewett and sentenced him to three years in prison, the scandal did not die down. Suspicious fires broke out at Peace Mission stores and farms, and angry crowds attacked Father Divine's followers on the streets of New York City.

In the spring of 1937, the police began to investigate Father Divine himself. At a Peace Mission rally in New York City, a crowd of followers beat two officials who tried to serve court papers on Father Divine. After the officers said Father Divine had ordered his followers to attack them, the preacher left the city and disappeared. Police soon found him hiding in the basement of a Peace Mission in Connecticut.

By this time, Faithful Mary had become a powerful leader in the Peace Mission movement. But instead of supporting Father Divine, she broke away from the group and formed her own spiritual community in upstate New York. Many of Divine's followers quit the Peace Mission to join her. Faithful Mary published *"God": He's Just a Natural Man*, a short book that accused Father Divine of bad faith and deception. According to Faithful Mary, Father Divine forced the Peace Missions and related businesses to make heavy payments to him. While he lived a

In 1940, Father Divine shows his followers to the Peace Mission's newly acquired, 500-acre "Heaven" estate, in Krumville, New York.

life of luxury, his followers worked long hours for low wages and slept in crowded rooms.

As the scandals continued, another former member of the Peace Mission filed a lawsuit against Father Divine. Verinda Brown claimed that Divine had taken her life's savings when she joined the church but had refused to give back the money after she left. Brown said Father Divine had fraudulently collected the money and diverted the organization's funds for his own use.

*Father Divine answers questions during a
New York City deposition concerning money
he allegedly swindled from his followers.*

In 1942, a New York court ruled in favor of Brown
and ordered Father Divine to repay her. The decision
meant that any of Father Divine's followers could now file
a similar suit—and win. If Father Divine returned
Brown's money, thousands of others who had contributed
their savings to the organization might demand refunds as
well, and the Peace Mission would face financial disaster.

60

Father Divine never paid Brown her settlement, but he realized he couldn't endure any more scandals or lawsuits. To improve the organization, he established new rules for the Peace Mission's angels, demanding that they wear uniforms, follow a strict code of behavior, and perform officially assigned duties. Divine now called his female followers "Rosebuds," and his male followers became "Crusaders." Rosebuds served as choir singers or secretaries, and Crusaders worked as guards or Peace Mission officers.

Next, Divine organized three official churches to carry out all Peace Mission activities and take ownership of homes and property. He placed all of the missions under central control and insisted that prospective missions apply for acceptance into the organization. Although the changes protected Father Divine from lawsuits, many of his followers felt cut off from their leader. Some left the Peace Mission movement permanently.

Still under the threat of arrest if he didn't pay Verinda Brown, Father Divine left New York in the summer of 1942 and settled in Philadelphia, where he was outside the jurisdiction of the New York courts. From time to time, he would return to New York to preach on Sundays—the only day of the week, according to New York law, that judges could not order him to appear in court.

Soon after his wife, Penninah, died, Father Divine began a romantic relationship with Edna Rose Hitchings, a young woman from Vancouver, Canada, who had joined the movement while still in high school. She had traveled to Pennsylvania to be near Father Divine and named herself Sweet Angel. After taking a job as a Peace Mission secretary, she proposed marriage to Father Divine. He accepted the proposal, then announced that his fiancée was the reincarnation of Penninah and the Virgin Mary. Father Divine christened Edna Hitchings the Spotless Virgin Bride, and the couple was married on April 29, 1946.

The wedding angered John Wuest Hunt, who was now free from jail and causing more problems for Father Divine. Hunt abandoned the Peace Mission and wrote a critical article for *Our World* magazine, calling his former spiritual leader a con man and declaring that the Peace Mission movement was a fraud. His accusations prompted the FBI to investigate the organization, but the agency found very little evidence of criminal activity and soon dropped the case.

In the 1950s, controversies surrounding the Peace Mission began to die down. No longer interested in politics, Divine returned to his first love—positive thinking and spiritual self-help. He moved the Peace Mission headquarters to Woodmont, a 72-acre estate in an exclusive suburb of Philadelphia. Woodmont had tennis courts, a swimming pool, riding stables, and spacious lawns. The estate's imposing mansion symbolized the

Peace Mission's prosperity and Father Divine's personal success.

In the early 1960s, with his health failing, Divine rarely left the estate and spent less time in public. Nevertheless, Peace Mission members all over the country still left an empty chair for him at the head of their banquet tables. On September 10, 1965, their leader died, but his wife—now known as the second Mother Divine—continued to lead the organization. Woodmont stayed open, and Peace Mission members from across the United States visited the estate. Mother Divine continued to hold banquets after her husband's death, but attendance fell sharply. By the 1990s, only a few branches of the church remained. Father Divine's philosophy has barely survived without him.

Science-fiction writer L. Ron Hubbard (1911-1986) told his fans that the Church of Scientology could cure their ailments and solve their problems. Many people outside the church, however, called Hubbard a fraud.

4

L. Ron Hubbard
The Church of Scientology

*T*hroughout history, most new religions have been formed when members break away from an established church. But writer L. Ron Hubbard broke this pattern by creating an entirely new religion and building a world-wide organization of fiercely loyal believers. Since the 1950s, millions of people have contributed their money and sacrificed much of their freedom for his creation, Scientology. Although Hubbard is now dead, the Church of Scientology lives on.

On March 13, 1911, La Fayette Ronald Hubbard was born in Tilden, Nebraska. The Hubbards moved to Montana when "Ron" was two. During World War I, Ron's father, Harry, began a lengthy career in the U.S. Navy. As the navy moved Harry Hubbard to new posts, his wife and son followed him to San Diego, Seattle, and Washington, D.C.

As a teenager, Ron Hubbard visited many exotic places. A long sea voyage in 1927 brought him to China and the Philippines. The following year, he spent several weeks with his family on the island of Guam. Determined to become a sailor, Hubbard requested a place in the U.S. Naval Academy, but he failed the entrance examination because of his poor skills in mathematics. In 1930, Ron decided to enroll in George Washington University in Washington, D.C., where he studied civil engineering. When he failed a physics course and did poorly in several other subjects, Hubbard dropped out after two years.

Although L. Ron Hubbard wasn't a successful student, he was a great storyteller. After leaving school, he earned money by writing wartime adventures, westerns, and detective stories. He even helped to write a 15-part movie serial called *The Secret of Treasure Island*. In 1937, he published his first hardcover book, *Buckskin Brigades*. The following year, he became a regular contributor to *Astounding Science Fiction*, one of the most popular fantasy magazines published at the time.

In 1941, as the United States prepared to enter World War II, Hubbard joined the naval reserves and eventually worked in one of the navy's public relations offices. Hubbard frequently suffered from fevers and eye problems and was often on the sick list. Because he also experienced bouts of depression and sometimes thought about killing himself, Hubbard once checked himself into a hospital for psychiatric treatment.

Desperate for money and a cure for his physical ailments and depression, Hubbard began working on a new treatment of his own. He called it "Dianetics," from a Greek word for the mind. This new system, Hubbard believed, would prevent mental illness, and make people healthier and more intelligent.

Dianetics was a method of counseling. By answering the questions of a special counselor, called an *auditor*, a patient would remember painful experiences. Hubbard claimed that these painful memories, or *engrams*, were the cause of all mental and physical illnesses. Eventually, auditing sessions would erase these engrams from people's minds and make them "clear," with total recall and flawless mental abilities.

John Campbell, the editor of *Astounding Science Fiction*, believed wholeheartedly in Dianetics. In the May 1950 issue of the magazine, Campbell published a lengthy article entitled "Dianetics: A New Science of the Mind." This was the first published description of Hubbard's new counseling method.

Shortly after the article appeared in print, Hubbard's book *Dianetics: The Modern Science of Mental Health* was published. The book offered a simple, easy-to-follow description of Dianetics. Because this new form of therapy didn't require doctors, extensive training, or a lot of money, it gained wide popularity. Promoted in the pages of *Astounding Science Fiction*, the book sold 150,000 copies during its first year of publication—the same number of copies that an average issue of *Astounding Science Fiction* sold.

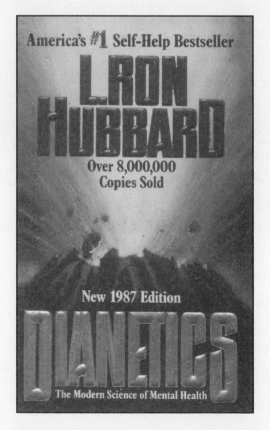

Dianetics: The Modern Science of Mental Health, *was first published in 1950. And, as this 1987 edition shows, the book has been popular ever since.*

Dianetics had succeeded beyond Hubbard's wildest expectations. Thousands of people, including some respected doctors and scientists, endorsed the new system. Fans set up Dianetics clubs, and people across the country tried Dianetics counseling on their friends and acquaintances.

Hubbard saw the Dianetics craze as a chance to set up a profitable business. But he was careful not to allow physicians and psychologists to use his methods and take control of his idea. In April 1950, just before *Dianetics* appeared in print, he had established the Hubbard Dianetic Research Foundation in Elizabeth, New Jersey. The foundation had a single purpose: to sell the Dianetics system. Through the foundation, Hubbard offered auditing sessions to the public for up to $25 an hour. Anyone who wanted to become a professional auditor could attend training sessions for a $500 fee.

As Hubbard's book hit the best-seller lists in the summer of 1950, new Dianetics foundations began operating in several major cities, including Los Angeles, New York, Honolulu, Chicago, and Washington, D.C. The foundations earned thousands of dollars every week from their patients and from counselors-in-training.

Hubbard made money by granting licenses to these businesses and taking a percentage of their income. But he kept little control over expenses and didn't bother to keep track of the large amount of money that was being earned. Hubbard grew suspicious of the people working for him and feared that many of the foundations were cheating him by keeping all of their profits or by inventing new methods of counseling to sell to the public.

Some of Hubbard's fears came true. One month, foundation employees could only account for $20,000 of the $90,000 they took in. After passing their training courses, many counselors left the foundation to set up their own Dianetics operations. Working without licenses, they kept all of the course fees for themselves. Worse, many doctors, psychologists, and journalists were openly doubting Hubbard's claims and beginning to criticize Dianetics.

Before long, Dianetics centers were losing clients and sinking into debt. John Campbell turned against Hubbard and resigned from the Hubbard Dianetic Research Foundation. Doctors who had endorsed Dianetics changed their minds and declared that recalling past memories probably wasn't enough to cure physical or mental illness. Moreover, many experts accused Hubbard of deceiving the public with a dangerous fraud.

Facing financial disaster in early 1951, Hubbard was relieved when a Kansas millionaire named Don Purcell offered Hubbard enormous financial support. Purcell, a strong believer in Hubbard's system, agreed to set up a new Dianetics foundation in Wichita, Kansas. Later that year, the foundation published Hubbard's next book, *The Science of Survival*, which described a method of exploring past lives during auditing. Hubbard's ideas on reincarnation interested his followers but quickly angered Purcell, who didn't believe in past lives. Because of this, Hubbard and his new sponsor argued bitterly over the future of their organization.

Although Purcell was supporting Dianetics with large sums of money, Hubbard soon changed his opinion about his new partner. Viewing the millionaire as a dangerous enemy, Hubbard stormed out of Wichita and attacked Purcell in a series of articles. The Wichita foundation soon went bankrupt, and Hubbard publicly accused Purcell of taking a bribe from the American Medical Association to destroy Dianetics.

Believing he was about to lose control of Dianetics, Hubbard devised a more elaborate system called Scientology. He used all of his skills as a science-fiction writer to create the system's rules and procedures. According to Scientology, each person's true self is an immortal being that has already lived for billions of years and has inhabited the far reaches of the universe. These beings—called *thetans*—have lived in millions of bodies but have gradually lost their many supernatural powers. The aim of auditing, Hubbard explained, was to restore these supernatural abilities and make the individual an "operating thetan."

Although Scientology sounded like something out of a science-fiction story to most people, many followers of Dianetics believed Hubbard's new theory. Nevertheless, Hubbard knew that he needed fresh techniques and innovations to draw in more customers. To give his clients a "scientific" impression of auditing, he created the electro-psychometer, or E-meter. People using this device held one tin can in each hand. A mild electric current passed along a wire between the cans and through the meter. A needle on the device supposedly detected changes in the current as it passed through the body.

Hubbard claimed that the E-meter could detect emotional changes in the person using it. Thus, the E-meter became a required purchase for anyone going through a Scientology auditing course, and Hubbard eventually began using the device to determine whether someone was lying. A certain reading on the E-meter allegedly showed an auditor that the subject was having unacceptable thoughts about Hubbard or Scientology.

To most people, Scientology and the fantastic abilities of the E-meter sounded completely ridiculous. Yet Hubbard, now the author of hundreds of articles and several more books about Scientology, managed to convince thousands of followers that he had discovered an entirely new realm of knowledge.

To protect his organization from taxes, bad publicity, and outside investigations, Hubbard also made Scientology a religion. He founded the first Church of Scientology in 1953 and later established more churches in the United States, Australia, and New Zealand. These churches operated as franchises and paid a portion of their profits to the California Church of Scientology, which then turned the money over to Hubbard.

The Scientology churches worked partly as businesses and partly as information centers. Dedicated Scientologists ran the centers according to Hubbard's detailed orders and instructions. Most of their income came from the sale of E-meters, books, and Scientology courses that promised to turn clients into "operating thetans."

The churches kept complete records of all auditing sessions. During these sessions, Scientology clients revealed details of their personal lives and described their private thoughts and feelings. The auditors listened carefully and encouraged their clients to associate only with other Scientologists.

As Hubbard designed a series of courses, each of which was more expensive than the last, followers of Scientology turned over more of their money and gave the church more control over their lives. Leaving the organization became increasingly difficult, and questioning Scientology became almost unthinkable.

During this period, Scientology gained many critics. Some claimed that Scientology, like Dianetics, was useless as a cure for physical or mental ailments. Others said that auditing was meant to turn normal people into obedient and unthinking followers of L. Ron Hubbard and his new church. Sure that his opponents were out to destroy him, Hubbard ordered his followers to harass, injure, or sue anyone who criticized his organization. He employed private detectives to investigate his critics, and the Church of Scientology also threatened and sued anyone who tried to set up independent Scientology centers.

By the late 1950s, the Scientology organization moved to Great Britain, where Dianetics had already attracted a small but loyal following. To attract followers, Hubbard used several new recruiting methods. One of the most effective was to advertise Scientology as a scientific research foundation that investigated cases of polio. People suffering from this illness volunteered as research subjects and signed up for auditing courses.

Hubbard earned a fortune as the money from Scientology franchises kept coming in. In 1959, he bought a British country estate called Saint Hill from a maharajah from India. Hubbard and his wife, Mary Sue, moved into the estate's spacious house and hired servants to wait on them. With new offices and classrooms, Saint Hill became an international training center for counselors and advanced Scientology students.

Despite his success, Hubbard was still convinced that his critics intended to destroy him. To increase his control over the growing organization, he appointed "ethics officers" to keep close watch over members and carry out harsh punishments for disloyalty. Through these officers, he encouraged Scientologists to spy on each other and to report anyone not teaching Scientology in the correct manner.

Having ethics officers earned Scientology bad publicity, however, especially in Great Britain and Australia. When newspaper writers criticized Scientology, the governments of both countries began investigating the church. In December 1965, the Australian state of Victoria officially banned Scientology. Claiming to be a victim of religious persecution, Hubbard simply changed the name of the Church of Scientology in Victoria to the Church of New Faith, and it survived. The following year, Britain's lawmakers prohibited Scientology members from entering the country, classified Hubbard as an "undesirable alien," and banned him from the nation. Nevertheless, Saint Hill continued to operate as the international Scientology center.

To hinder any future investigations, Hubbard created a top-secret Scientology department called the Guardian's Office. He put his wife, Mary Sue, in charge of the new office, which gathered information on people or agencies that Hubbard regarded as enemies. In the United States, members of the Guardian's Office broke into several government departments in Washington, D.C., including the Justice Department and the Internal Revenue Service.

Convinced that the world's governments had hatched an elaborate conspiracy against him, Hubbard formally resigned as the president of the Church of

Scientology in 1966. Although he continued to write books and instructions for the Scientology branches, he claimed that he was no longer earning money from the organization.

To escape the many investigations of his church and put himself outside the laws of Britain, Australia, and any other country, Hubbard established the "Sea Organization" in the late 1960s. He bought the *Royal Scotsman*, a converted cattle ferry, and selected a small group of young and loyal Scientologists to operate the ship. Calling himself the "commodore," Hubbard issued uniforms to his crew and set sail.

Although members of the Sea Organization were close to their leader, they were also subject to tough discipline. Mistakes and disobedience led to confinement in the ship's dark and dirty cargo holds. A false word or a slip-up in carrying out Hubbard's orders sometimes led to the punishment of "overboarding," at which point crew members tied up their disobedient colleagues with ropes, then threw them over the side of the ship for a few minutes before hauling them back on deck.

For several years, the *Royal Scotsman* (which Hubbard renamed the *Apollo*) sailed in the eastern Atlantic Ocean and in the Mediterranean Sea. The ship voyaged from port to port, anchoring for a few weeks or months in a single harbor. Hubbard continued to hold Scientology courses and lectures on the ship, which became a floating command center for the organization.

By the late 1960s, L. Ron Hubbard, who was not welcome in several countries, suspected that some of his supporters were trying to sabotage the Church of Scientology.

Hubbard saw his voyage as a way of spreading Scientology around the world. But officials in Greece, Morocco, Portugal, and several other nations did not appreciate the strange behavior of the *Apollo* crew. Some countries posted guards near the ship to prevent contact between crew members and the local population or barred the *Apollo* from entering their harbors altogether.

In the early 1970s, Hubbard grew tired of his life at sea and made plans to go ashore in the United States. To avoid investigation by the press or the FBI, he set up an organization called the United Churches of Florida, which did not publicly disclose its ties to Scientology.

Through the United Churches, Scientologists bought a large hotel, a local bank, and several apartment buildings in Clearwater, Florida. In 1975, the Clearwater properties became the new headquarters for Scientology.

By the time he left the *Apollo*, Hubbard had recruited several sons and daughters of Scientology followers into the Commodore's Messenger Organization (CMO), which was responsible for relaying Hubbard's messages and orders to the rest of the ship. After leaving the *Apollo*, Hubbard began to cut himself off from the outside world. He avoided his friends and grew even more fearful and suspicious of his critics. At the same time, the CMO became the most powerful group within the church.

Meanwhile, the Guardian's Office began to suffer the consequences of its activities. The U.S. government apprehended two spies from the Guardian's Office who were trying to steal files from federal agencies in Washington, D.C. As a result of the investigation that followed, the government arrested Mary Sue Hubbard in 1979. On September 24, she was found guilty of stealing federal documents and burglarizing government offices. She was fined $10,000 and spent a year and a half in prison. Claiming he knew nothing of his wife's activities, L. Ron Hubbard managed to escape prosecution.

During the early 1980s, the CMO gradually took over the leadership of the Church of Scientology. In May 1981, the leader of the CMO, 21-year-old David

Miscavige, took action to weaken the Scientology franchises. Threatening the Scientology centers with the loss of their profits and their franchises, he forced the owners of these centers to sign new contracts, which meant paying larger franchise fees and following very strict guidelines for course offerings and auditing.

To ensure that each Scientology center was loyal, Miscavige also sent out teams of spies to check on the franchises. Any Scientology teacher guilty of violating the guidelines had to report to a Scientology center and undergo a security check. Because they did not want to lose their businesses—some of which brought in as much as $100,000 every week—most franchise owners accepted the new conditions. But others lost faith in L. Ron Hubbard and left the church.

At this time, Hubbard was living secretly with a handful of young aides from the Commodore's Messenger Organization. Moving from place to place in the deserts of southern California, he stopped all communication with his family and friends. Many Scientologists believed that their leader was dead and that the CMO and David Miscavige had completely taken over the church. None of them knew that Hubbard was suffering from heart trouble and many other serious illnesses. Although Hubbard had claimed that his courses could rid people of illnesses, he died of a stroke in January 1986 on a remote ranch in California.

Popular actors Tom Cruise and Kirstie Alley have spoken publicly about how Scientology has improved their lives.

Today, Scientology remains a wealthy organization, with properties and training centers all over the world. It has fought off several investigations by the Internal Revenue Service, and U.S. courts have declared it to be a tax-exempt religious organization. New followers sign up every day, and the church has enlisted well-known celebrities to follow its courses and promote the organization. The price of courses, auditing sessions, books, and tapes runs into tens of thousands of dollars. For many people, however, the promise that Hubbard held out—the chance to attain the elusive state of "clear"—is well worth the cost.

According to Sun Myung Moon, the only reason people distrust him is "because my skin is yellow." Moon, the founder of the Unification Church, has been accused of "brainwashing" his followers.

82

5

Sun Myung Moon
The Unification Church

Korea was a troubled land in the early twentieth century. Japan, a powerful empire and Korea's eastern neighbor across the Sea of Japan, occupied the country. Japan imposed its laws and industries on the Koreans, then gave Korean land to new settlers from the Japanese islands. The Koreans weren't strong enough to drive out the Japanese, but some Koreans realized they could resist the Japanese occupation through religion.

Yong Myung Moon, a man who would eventually lead a church of international prominence, was born on January 6, 1920, into a poor farming family in northern

Korea. When he was ten, Yong Myung's family converted to Presbyterianism. Religion became important to Moon, who drew strength and inspiration from the sermons he heard in church.

While he was still in high school, he began reporting powerful visions. Yong Myung claimed that on Easter Sunday in 1936, Jesus Christ, the Son of God, appeared to him and told him to establish a heavenly kingdom on earth where people would love one another. During the

Christians believe that Jesus Christ (seated, in white robe) performed miracles, such as healing the sick and rising from the dead.

84

next few years, Moon prayed and meditated on his future. He said that visions of Moses and Buddha appeared to guide him. Gradually, he decided to establish and lead a new Christian church.

When the Allied forces defeated Japan in World War II, the occupation of Korea ended. But the country split into two separate and hostile governments. A Communist government, supported by the Soviet Union, ruled North Korea, while South Korea allied itself with the United States.

Moon, who had studied electrical engineering at Waseda University in Japan, journeyed to Pyongyang, a city in northern Korea, in 1943. When World War II ended two years later, he founded the Kwang Ya Church, where his preaching began to attract a small congregation. Soon afterward, he decided to change his name to Sun Myung Moon.

While Moon was living in Pyongyang, the two Korean nations built a fortified border that divided the north from the south. North of the barrier, the Communist regime proclaimed that North Korea was now an atheist state that would prohibit religious worship. The North Korean officials arrested Moon in 1946 and again in 1948. The North Korean government closed down the Kwang Ya Church and sent its leader to a labor camp for five years.

In 1950, war broke out between North and South Korea. In October, South Korean soldiers freed Moon and several of his followers from prison. Moon fled to the South Korean port of Pusan, where he found a job as a dock worker in 1951. There, he was free to establish another church and openly express his theological beliefs. In the early 1950s Reverend Moon set down his religious ideas in a lengthy essay entitled *The Divine Principle*.

One of the main topics of Moon's book was humankind's fall into sin and disobedience, which is described in Genesis, the first book of the Bible. Moon divided people into two opposing types that could be traced back to Adam and Eve, the first two people God created, and their first two sons, Cain and Abel.

Sun Myung Moon, who preached that communism was evil, had been deeply troubled by the Korean War, which began in 1950 when Communist forces from North Korea invaded South Korea.

(According to the Bible, Cain resented and eventually murdered his brother Abel, whom God had favored.) The "Abel-types," according to Moon, represented divinity, while the "Cain-types" represented evil. Moon believed the world would eventually see a final, deadly struggle between good and evil.

Moon said he intended to lead the fight by unifying the world's Christian believers against the evil forces of the devil. In May 1954, Moon founded the Holy Spirit Association for the Unification of World Christianity, usually referred to as the Unification Church. The Unification Church initially included only Moon and a handful of his followers, but the church soon grew.

Larger churches and congregations in South Korea criticized and ridiculed Moon's religious sect. Korea's Presbyterian Church, which did not believe in visions and revelations, had already expelled him. Moon's message, however, appealed to many people. When a professor from the Ewha Women's University in Tokyo came to investigate the new Unification Church, Moon quickly converted her to his beliefs. Soon many other students and professors from the school joined Moon's religious family. In 1957, *The Divine Principle* was published as a book. That year, a loyal follower and English-speaking scholar named Young Oon Kim (often called Miss Kim) translated Moon's book into English.

Because of the book and the recruiting effort, the Unification Church grew steadily with new members joining every day. Moon began sending missionaries to convert Christians in other Korean cities to his church. Moon realized that he could build a worldwide church, so he looked to other nations for more converts.

Sang Ik Choi, a devoted aide, secretly moved from Korea to Japan in 1958 to recruit young college students. To attract and keep new members, the Unification Church of Japan developed a strict system of guidance. Members of the church lived together under a single roof, and all activities—sleeping, eating, exercise, discussions, and worship—took place at a scheduled time. The church shielded its members from contact with the outside world and enforced unquestioning loyalty to Reverend Moon and his doctrines.

At this point, Young Oon Kim enrolled at the University of Oregon and began preaching *The Divine Principle* to the students she met there. She gathered new members of the church in a small group that she called the "Unified Family."

Moon provided little guidance to Miss Kim or his other missionaries, who brought new members into the church any way they could. This task proved especially difficult in foreign countries, where the Korean customs and language were unfamiliar. By the time Miss Kim moved to California in 1960, she had converted only a small number of people. But copies of *The Divine Principle* that she had passed out in the United States won over six Germans who were living in the United States at the time. Moon was pleased when they returned to Germany to start new missionary centers.

In 1965, Miss Kim moved the Unified Family to Washington D.C. Sang Ik Choi traveled from Japan to take her place in California, where he quickly built the largest Moon family in the United States. Many young people, seeking a life free of day-to-day worries, joined the group. In return for security and guidance, they adopted Moon's religion and accepted Sang Ik Choi's strict control of their daily lives.

In the late 1960s, however, Moon's Unification Church was just one among many new religious sects in the United States. Moon gained little public notice until 1969, when the Washington, D.C., branch of the church established the Freedom Leadership Foundation, which organized demonstrations and fasts in support of the Vietnam War. As the demonstrations attracted larger crowds and the church converted many new members, the U.S. press and the public began paying attention to the church.

Moon's support of U.S. involvement in the Vietnam War reflected his belief that his church had an important role to play in world events. He saw the struggle against communism as part of the struggle against evil. Moon also believed that the United States was the only country in the world strong enough to defeat communism. For that reason, he sought to influence the U.S.

government through the Unification Church in Washington, D.C.

In 1971, Moon arrived in the United States for his third international tour to promote the Unification Church. He spoke through a translator at arenas and auditoriums across the country, calling on his audiences to abandon their old religious beliefs and join the church. Soon afterward, Moon became a permanent resident of the United States, and this greatly boosted the church's membership there.

To pay for Moon's speaking tours, his followers sold flowers and religious soundtracks in airports, bus stations, and other public places. The church bought Belvedere, an estate in Tarrytown, New York, where Moon established the Unification Theological Seminary, which became a training center for future leaders of the church.

Moon worked quickly to make powerful friends in the nation's capital. In 1973, when President Richard Nixon was facing a congressional investigation concerning his involvement in the Watergate burglary, Moon publicly supported the president. That year, the Washington, D.C., branch of the Unification Church announced that its members would go on a 40-day fast in support of Nixon.

As part of a $72,000 pro-Nixon media campaign, the church paid for full-page advertisements in major newspapers, asking people to forgive the president and to unite behind him in the fight against communism. Nixon

The Unification Church received national attention, and new members, by supporting President Richard Nixon (1913-1994) during the Watergate scandal. Nixon served as president from 1969 to 1974.

showed his gratitude by inviting Moon to the White House for a meeting. Although the Watergate scandal led Nixon to resign in 1974, Moon had gained valuable publicity for his organization.

The leaders of the church gradually developed a reliable method to win new recruits in the United States. Dressed neatly and speaking politely, members of the church struck up conversations with young adults, especially college students who were living away from their families. Without mentioning Moon directly, his followers claimed they were forming a cooperative world community. Eventually, they extended an invitation to a special dinner to introduce outsiders to the Unification

91

Church. Friendly faces greeted the guests and encouraged them to discuss Moon's doctrines. Then, members of the church would invite interested visitors to attend a workshop in a rural area or at an isolated campsite.

Out of curiosity, many of the guests agreed to attend the workshop. For a few days, they stayed with a close group of friends who ate, talked, and exercised together. A group leader escorted the visitors at all times and monitored their activities. In discussion groups, the leaders announced the topics of conversation, but discouraged visitors from talking informally to one another.

Eventually, the group leaders invited the visitors to join the Moon family. If the visitors accepted, they gave their personal possessions and their money to the church and gradually lost contact with family and friends. The Unification Church became their new family, providing them with food, clothing, and shelter.

The Unification Church trained its members to be hostile toward the outside world and to keep their distance from it. Moon became a father figure for his followers, many of whom had suffered from frustration or loneliness before they joined the church. He convinced his followers that people who were not "Moonies"—an informal name for members of the Unification Church— were evil. According to Moon, any of his followers who left the church and returned to the outside world would be possessed by the devil.

In return for membership in Moon's family, the church expected the recruits to solicit money from people in airports and other public places. After three years of devoted service and fundraising, and after bringing three new recruits into the Unification Church, Moonies won the reverend's personal blessing and were free to marry a spouse that the church selected for them. Since 1960, Sun Myung Moon himself had been married to one of his followers, Hak Ja Han.

Nearly 800 couples are married at a mass wedding for Unification Church members in Seoul, South Korea, in 1970.

In 1974, the Unification Church had more than 25,000 members in the United States and more than 1 million members in both Japan and Korea. But by the late 1970s, U.S. newspapers and magazines had published many critical articles about the church, and parents had begun to complain about the church's recruitment of their children. Many people accused Moon of robbing his followers of their freedom to act and to think for themselves. In 1977, a California judge ordered five young adults to leave the cult and return to the custody of their parents, saying that Moon had "brainwashed" them.

Moon also drew unwanted attention from government agencies, including the Internal Revenue Service, which is responsible for collecting taxes. The IRS and the Justice Department began to investigate Moon's political work in Washington, D.C. Moon also made newspaper headlines in 1978, when many members of the U.S. Congress were accused of taking bribes from the government of South Korea.

To fight the bad publicity, Moon set up new organizations backed by money from his church. The Council for Unified Research and Education sponsored annual scientific meetings, the Korean Folk Ballet performed Korean folk dances around the world, and the Collegiate Association for the Research of Principles held meetings on college campuses.

Meanwhile, money from donations kept flowing into the church's many bank accounts. The Unification

Church bought factories, set up export companies, and made investments around the world. In addition, the organization bought the *Washington Times*, the second largest newspaper in Washington, D.C. Moon also spent $48 million to produce *Inchon*, a movie about the Korean War, which starred internationally known actor Laurence Olivier as General Douglas MacArthur.

Investigations into the Unification Church led the federal government to bring Moon to trial in late 1981. The IRS accused him of failing to pay $150,000 in taxes between 1973 and 1976. Lawyers for the church argued that the money belonged to a religious organization and was, therefore, nontaxable. In his defense, Moon also claimed that the government was discriminating against him because of his race and his religion. The Church of Jesus Christ of Latter-day Saints and several other religious organizations supported him.

But Moon lost the case. In July 1982, a federal court sentenced him to 18 months in prison and ordered him to pay a fine of $25,000. The Unification Church appealed the decision but lost again. Moon served his jail term, and he was deported from the United States following his release in 1985.

Moon's trial and the many newspaper investigations had brought the Unification Church bad publicity, and the organization began losing members. Many recruits in the United States and Europe, where criticism and questioning of authority were more common than in Asia,

Unification Church supporters rally in New York City to support Sun Myung Moon, who was charged with tax evasion in 1981.

could not adapt to the church's demand of absolute loyalty. Unification centers closed down, and Moonies no longer appeared on the streets to ask for donations. Recruiting on college campuses ended.

After leaving the United States, Moon settled in South Korea, where he turned his attention away from religion and toward business. He had already built an economic empire there. His manufacturing companies made consumer goods and industrial supplies. He owned media companies, and he supported schools, seminaries, orchestras, and a ballet company. The Unification Church had turned away from its early goal of unifying the world's Christian believers, but it had become a wealthy organization.

Although Moon continued preaching against communism, he invested in Communist China and met with Soviet president Mikhail Gorbachev. Moon also sent missionaries into China, the Soviet Union, and North Korea. Moon said that if communism fell in North Korea, he would make his church a powerful influence in that country, where he had founded his first church in the 1940s. Moon has also begun to prepare his wife and his aides to run the Unification Church's powerful international businesses long after his death.

Peoples Temple leader Jim Jones (1931-1978), who often wore sunglasses in public, told his followers to distrust the outside world.

6

Jim Jones
The Peoples Temple

*J*im Jones inspired a strange kind of faith in his followers. He rarely mentioned the Bible or preached a religious sermon, but he could make people trust him and
believe in his ability to help them or cause harm to others.
Under his direction, the followers of Jim Jones gave up
their money, their belongings, and eventually their lives.

James Jones was born on May 13, 1931, in Crete,
Indiana. Jim's family moved to the nearby town of Lynn
when he was an infant. His father was a construction
worker and a member of the Ku Klux Klan. His mother

worked in a factory and believed in spirits and enchant-
ments. She and young Jim attended the local Church of
the Nazarene, which had split from the Methodist
Church during the 1800s.

Church rituals and sermons fascinated Jim, and he
became a serious student of the Bible. In his free time, he
led his own small congregation of neighborhood
children, pretending to baptize his friends and holding
funerals for their pets. As a teenager, Jim Jones began
delivering rousing sermons on street corners and worked
as an orderly at a local hospital. Soon after enrolling at
Indiana University in Bloomington, Jones married a
hospital nurse named Marceline Baldwin. In the early
1950s, Jones combined his interests in religion and med-
icine and claimed to be a "faith healer" who could cure
people through preaching rather than by prescribing
medication.

After moving to Indianapolis in 1951, Jones joined
the Sommerset Methodist Church as a student pastor.
The church welcomed people of all faiths, and Jones's
sermons attracted large crowds every Sunday morning.
The elders of the Sommerset Methodist Church appreci-
ated the new members and their donations, and Jones
loved the attention and the praise of his congregation.
But he quickly grew tired of preaching in somebody else's
church and wanted to lead a congregation of his own.

Jones got the chance to head his own church when
the Sommerset Methodist Church split into two hostile

Although his father had been a member of the racist Ku Klux Klan, Jim Jones preached racial equality.

factions, with whites and blacks angry with each other. Because Jones preached racial equality, many of his most fervent supporters were black. He decided to leave the Sommerset Church and move to a different part of Indianapolis. There he rented a small building and named it the Community Unity Church.

Jim Jones filled the pews of the Community Unity Church every Sunday. His powerful voice convinced listeners that he could cure diseases and disabilities. Even people who didn't believe in such miracles came to listen to Jones's message about *one* human race, in which everyone was equal in the eyes of God.

By 1955, Jones had collected enough money to buy a church of his own on the north side of Indianapolis.

He called it the Peoples Temple Full Gospel Church, and every Sunday he held three services. Unlike most of the city's other churches, the Peoples Temple was fully integrated. Whites and blacks prayed together and mixed freely in the pews and aisles. Jones worked hard to make his church an important part of the surrounding neighborhood. He set up a soup kitchen for the hungry and collected clothing for the poor. Soon, every churchgoer in the city knew about the Peoples Temple.

Despite his success, Jones remained restless and unsatisfied. Running a church was expensive, and Jones and his wife barely scraped by on the donations from his congregation. He needed new members and new ideas. Jones became inspired by the Peace Mission movement led by Father Divine. In 1956, he traveled to Pennsylvania to visit one of the missions and learn more about the organization.

After returning to Indianapolis, Jones purchased a Jewish synagogue that could seat 400 people. Gradually, he assumed more control over the lives of his followers. He expected them to appear at church functions several times a week and to make large, regular contributions to the church's treasury.

With the increased donations, Jones hired several aides to help him keep track of his congregation. They asked members of the congregation to turn in a list of their fears and personal problems, and Jones ordered his aides to sift through garbage cans secretly to learn more about members of the congregation. Jones would work this information into his sermons, calling on his members by name and revealing these intimate facts as if they were divine revelations.

Jones suffered from a deep fear of betrayal and couldn't stand the thought of anyone leaving his church. To maintain control, he asked his aides to insult and threaten anyone who tried to leave the Peoples Temple. Many of Jones's followers began to fear their leader, whose actions and words were becoming unpredictable and frightening.

At one service, Jones announced that he had received a revelation that a nuclear holocaust would destroy the Midwest. Obsessed with finding a safe refuge

Jim Jones, who feared the Midwest would be bombed by nuclear warheads, desperately wanted to move the Peoples Temple out of Indianapolis.

for the Peoples Temple, he traveled for more than a year during the early 1960s to find a new home for his church. Jones visited several locations in South America, which he thought would be safe from the mass destruction he foretold.

After returning to Indianapolis, Jones said he had a vision that the Peoples Temple should relocate to California. In 1965, he moved his family and about 150 members of his congregation to Ukiah, a small town north of San Francisco. In Ukiah, the Peoples Temple faced new problems. Having no church building, the congregation held religious services on nearby fairgrounds and later in Jones's garage.

The congregation survived by working together. To help pay the bills, Jones taught evening classes for adults in a local school. After finding jobs, the church members turned over their earnings to Jones and built a new church in their free time. The Peoples Temple later established a ranch for mentally handicapped boys, homes for the elderly, a day-care center, and foster homes for children. Money from U.S. government agencies, which went to support public health efforts, enabled the church to offer these services.

At this time, Jones's strong opinions were attracting public attention. After he led a march against the Vietnam War through the streets of Ukiah, many people who agreed with Jones's political views joined the Peoples Temple. Jones also won new members through his evening classes, in which he harshly criticized the U.S. government.

In his sermons, Jones spoke more and more about politics and current events. He eventually stopped reading from the Bible because, he said, the book was racist and promoted slavery. Jones sometimes threw the Bible to the floor and stomped on it in anger. By now, he had concluded that the capitalist system in the United States was a failure and that the Peoples Temple should support socialism. Members of the congregation donated all of their money and their possessions to the group. In return, the church provided them with shelter, food, and medical care.

Jones believed that the U.S. government posed a grave threat to his small church. To prepare for potential attacks from the Federal Bureau of Investigation and the Central Intelligence Agency, the Peoples Temple held regular "survival drills." Members of the congregation built remote hideouts in the hills surrounding Ukiah and collected canned food, bottled water, and medical supplies in readiness for the coming battle.

At the same time, Jones and his followers were driving into San Francisco and winning converts in the city's poorer neighborhoods. As the organization grew to more than 1,000 members, Jones asked several of his most trusted aides to join a church police force. This "Planning Commission" made sure everyone attended services and followed the strict rules of the organization.

Members of the Peoples Temple had to obtain the approval of the commission to apply for a job, rent an apartment, buy a car, get married, or have children.

In 1970, Jones conducted the marriage service for Timothy and Grace Stoen, two of his most devoted followers. But his involvement with the Stoen family did not end there. When the couple had their first child two years later, Jones demanded that Timothy Stoen sign a document falsely stating that Jones was the baby's real father, giving him custody of their son.

Convinced that unseen enemies wanted to kill him, Jones posted armed guards at the church doors 24 hours a day and treated all visitors, especially reporters, with suspicion. He also used look-alikes as decoys whenever he appeared in public, and his behavior was becoming more erratic. Still, Jones promised that, in time, he could cure his followers of cancer, blindness, and other medical problems, and they remained dedicated to him.

His fears growing, Jones organized a new church ritual—the "suicide drill." In this ceremony, he ordered church members to drink a dark liquid, which he said was poison. After a few minutes, the drill ended, with the congregation still alive. Jones would then announce that his followers had just been through a test of their loyalty. In case an actual mass suicide ever became necessary, however, Jones forced his aides to sign a statement explaining why they were killing themselves.

In 1972, Jones bought a church in San Francisco and started additional social programs in the community. Because many of the strange and sinister occurrences in the church remained secret from the outside world, most non-members thought the Peoples Temple was a caring church. For this reason, San Franciscans gave Jones and his followers a warm welcome. Although membership at the Temple never grew much higher than 3,000, crowds of up to 100,000 people would come to hear Jones speak in public.

The Temple also set up an agricultural project in the jungles of Guyana, a small country in South America. Jones called this project "The Promised Land" after the farming commune in New York started by his idol, Father Divine. The Peoples Temple leased approximately 3,000 acres of land from the Guyanese government. The land was located near the town of Port Kaituma, about 150 miles from the capital city of Georgetown. In June 1974, the first Temple members from San Francisco arrived to clear the jungle and prepare the ground for plowing and planting. Many of these pioneers were young men suffering hard times or in trouble with the law.

This work on behalf of the poor in San Francisco earned Jones powerful friends in the city's government. The Temple had become an influential political organization because Jones could order his followers to gather for demonstrations, register voters, or send out mass mailings during a political campaign. In 1975, the support of the Peoples Temple helped George Moscone to win the election for mayor. He was the first liberal mayor the city had had in several years, and he won by only a few hundred votes.

Local papers and television news stations, however, began to present some unflattering stories about the Peoples Temple. San Franciscans heard repeated rumors of beatings, kidnappings, and child abuse in the church. The news stories described the church's financial dealings, as well as the rules, regulations, and punishments of the Planning Commission.

As his suspicion of the outside world continued to grow, Jones turned his fears against his followers. Anyone breaking church rules now faced a severe beating in front of the congregation. He also forced those he suspected of disloyalty to fight against bigger and stronger opponents in boxing matches. The church punished misbehaving children with stern lectures and physical abuse.

The punishments drove several members out of the church, but those who left still lived with fear. Members of the Planning Commission would sometimes come to their homes at night to scold them. Jones said that anyone who publicly criticized the organization would die. Some former members did meet mysterious deaths, which at first looked like accidents or suicides. Before these "accidents," Jones would announce to the congregation that his avenging angels were about to strike one of his enemies.

Most members of the Peoples Temple could not leave, however, because they depended on the church for everything they had. Fear and exhaustion broke their will to resist. Accepting Jones's word, the members believed that the U.S. government and the press were out to destroy the Peoples Temple. To leave the church or to criticize their preacher in any way became an almost unthinkable act of betrayal.

Nevertheless, in the summer of 1977, several former members began talking to reporters about the Peoples Temple. That year, two writers from *New West* magazine investigated the group and discovered that the rumors of intimidation and beatings were true. The writers also spoke to Grace Stoen, who had left the church and was

Grace Stoen tells reporters about "suicide drills" and other strange practices within the Peoples Temple.

now trying to get her son out of the Peoples Temple and away from Jim Jones. Her husband, Timothy Stoen, had also defected.

After the *New West* article was published, Jones feared an investigation of his church by U.S. authorities and moved the 1,000 members of his church to Guyana. Since 1974, several dozen members of the Peoples Temple

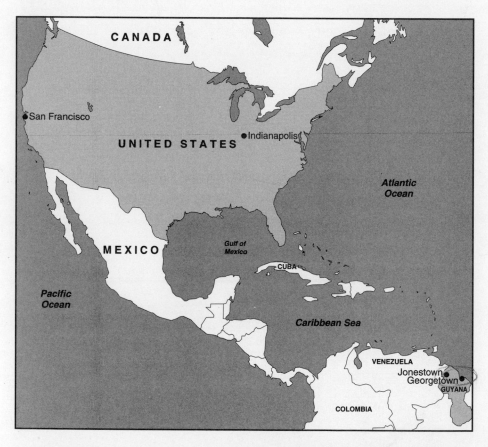

Afraid that outsiders would endanger the Peoples Temple, Jim Jones relocated his congregation from Indiana, to California, and then to the jungles of Guyana, approximately 1,000 miles from U.S. shores.

110

*With his wife, Marceline, at his side, Jim Jones
preaches to his congregation in Jonestown, Guyana.*

had built houses and dormitories in the jungle, along
with a large pavilion for services, a clinic, a day-care center, a radio shack, a guard tower, and an ammunition
shed. Jones claimed that the settlement, which the
Guyanese called Jonestown, would soon be a
self–supporting, socialist paradise. Armed guards
watched the gates to the community and patrolled the
nearby roads and footpaths. Dangerous snakes and
cougars roamed the jungle that surrounded the compound, making escape on foot impossible.

Jones did not allow visits from outsiders, but this did not keep Grace and Timothy Stoen from trying to regain custody of their son. After a San Francisco court granted the Stoens' request to have their child returned, the Guyanese courts ordered Jones to appear in Georgetown.

When he heard about the order, Jones flew into a rage and announced that unless the court changed its mind, every resident of Jonestown would commit suicide. Because of this, the Guyanese government backed out of the case, and the Stoen custody battle became the responsibility of the U.S. government.

At the same time, the reports on the Peoples Temple in *New West* and in the *San Francisco Chronicle* were prompting investigations of the group. Families of Temple members formed a group called the Concerned Relatives, which asked U.S. authorities to help them to get their loved ones out of Jonestown.

In early 1978, Leo Ryan, a California congressman, decided to meet with the Concerned Relatives. After hearing the stories about the Peoples Temple, Ryan agreed to fly to Guyana and visit Jonestown. He promised that anyone wishing to leave the compound would be able to do so under his protection.

That autumn, Ryan contacted Jim Jones and announced that he would travel to Guyana in November. Although the Peoples Temple tried to discourage the visit, Ryan insisted. On November 17, 1978, he arrived in Georgetown with several aides, 14 members of the

112

California congressman Leo Ryan arrived in Jonestown in November 1978 to check reports that U.S. citizens were being held prisoner in the jungles of Guyana.

Concerned Relatives, and newspaper and television reporters.

To Jones, Ryan's visit was another government attack on the Peoples Temple. With the media investigations and Leo Ryan's visit, the pressure was growing hard for him to bear. Several times he gathered his followers in the Jonestown pavilion, where he shouted angrily through the night. He imprisoned members of the congregation in their dormitories. Others were drugged or mercilessly beaten for the smallest violation of the rules. The suicide drills became more frequent.

In Georgetown, the congressman announced that he would escort anyone wishing to leave Jonestown out of the country. A cameraman and reporter from the NBC television network would record the entire

113

operation. Thus, if Jones refused to cooperate, a national television audience in the United States would witness his actions and would pressure the Guyanese government to close down Jonestown.

Ryan and his group chartered two small planes to fly to the nearby town of Port Kaituma. After the one-hour flight from Georgetown, the group was met by several Jonestown guards. Jones's wife, Marceline, showed the visitors around the community. Realizing that he had to meet Ryan, Jones ordered members of the Peoples Temple to prepare food and music for their guests. Several members gave interviews, all claiming to be happy at the compound. But the atmosphere grew tense after one member passed a note to Don Harris, the NBC reporter, asking for help in getting out of Guyana.

Jones gave Ryan and the reporters a friendly tour of Jonestown the next day. But when a total of 14 people asked for help in leaving, the leader and his guards turned hostile. At one point, a young member of the compound rushed at Ryan with a knife. Another member of the Peoples Temple grabbed the attacker and accidentally gave him a deep cut with the knife. Blood splashed on the front of the congressman's shirt. Growing fearful, Ryan said that everyone who wanted to leave should head back to Port Kaituma, where the planes awaited them. Several members of the Peoples Temple decided to join him.

Jones believed that these defections would lead to more defections. Eventually, his followers would simply

114

leave him, one by one, until he was left alone in the jungle. Jonestown—The Promised Land—would come to an end. The leader of the Peoples Temple wouldn't allow his dream to perish. He ordered Larry Layton, one of his aides, to board the plane carrying the defectors and shoot the pilot once the plane was airborne. That way, the plane would crash, and no one who left the church would survive.

Ryan left for the Port Kaituma airstrip with his aides, the reporters, and the Jonestown defectors, who pleaded with Ryan not to allow Larry Layton to join them. But the congressman said that Layton could come along. Three Jonestown guards, armed with loaded shotguns, followed the group in a truck to Port Kaituma, where two planes waited with their engines running.

After arriving at the airstrip, Ryan and his aides arranged the passenger seating on each plane and prepared for their flight. Within a few minutes, the Jonestown guards arrived. As their truck pulled up to the side of the airstrip, they leapt onto the ground, approached the planes, and opened fire. The congressman, one Jonestown defector, an NBC cameraman, and two other journalists were killed. The NBC camera, which kept running even after its operator lay dead on the airstrip, captured the scene on videotape.

The murderers quickly returned to Jonestown and told Jim Jones what had happened. Jones decided that the murder of a U.S. congressman and four others had brought the Peoples Temple to the end of its journey. He ordered several nurses to prepare a large vat of punch and pour in a lethal dose of potassium cyanide and other poisons.

The aides and the nurses gathered the people of Jonestown together in the big pavilion. Jim Jones announced to his congregation that the compound would soon be coming under direct attack. Jones called out to his followers to line up and drink the deadly poison. Children and babies went first, followed by the adults. Those who resisted were held down by guards and given injections. This was no drill.

A few people escaped into the surrounding jungle, but 914 of Jones's followers—including almost 300 children—died in agony. Unable to bring himself to drink the punch, Jones took an overdose of drugs. He was still alive when one of Jones's followers put a bullet through his head. The bodies lay motionless in the jungle for a full day before the news reached Georgetown and the outside world.

"Hurry, my children, hurry," Jim Jones *told his followers as they drank the poison that ended their lives.*

Prabhupada (1896-1977), who brought "Krishna Consciousness" to the United States, leads a group of chanting followers in New York City.

7

Prabhupada
The Hare Krishnas

*N*ew York City—sometimes called the business and entertainment capital of the world—is known for its interesting sites and creative people. Visitors from across the globe walk down the busy streets of New York every day, and most New Yorkers pay little attention to these newcomers.

But on September 19, 1965, a little-known man arrived in the hectic metropolis, hoping to draw attention to himself and his beliefs. He was thin and bald, with clay marks on his face, and he wore sandal-like slippers and a flowing cape. His few possessions included some cooking utensils, and a meager seven dollars. The man was Abhay Caranavinda Bhaktivedanta Swami Prabhupada, of Calcutta, India, and he had travelled 10,000 miles to bring Lord Krishna, a Hindu deity, to the United States.

Prabhupada's journey had begun 69 years before, when he was born as Abhay Charan De. A talented student, he had attended the Scottish Church College in Calcutta, one of India's best colleges. After graduating, he became the manager of a pharmaceutical company, married, and raised five children. But he was unsatisfied.

Seeking a deeper meaning for his life, Abhay Charan De studied the Bhagavad-Gita, an epic poem written in the ancient language of Sanskrit and an important part of the Hindu scripture. The poem consists of a dialogue between Prince Arjuna, a warrior preparing for a great battle, and his chariot-driver, Krishna, a manifestation of Vishnu, one of the chief gods of Hinduism. By teaching him to be selfless and instructing him in spirituality, Krishna gives Arjuna strength for the coming battle.

In the centuries after the Bhagavad-Gita (which means "Song of the Lord") was written, the poem inspired many different religious sects in India. In the sixteenth century, a group devoted to the public worship of Krishna formed in Bengal, a region of northeastern India. The members wore simple clothes, ate their meals together, and danced in public places while chanting their devotion to Krishna.

Nearly 400 years later, Abhay Charan De met a holy man named Bhaktisiddhanta Sarasvati Goswami. This scholar was a fundamentalist who believed in the literal truth of the events described in the Bhagavad-Gita. In 1933, he initiated Abhay as a *swami,* or teacher. Goswami encouraged his dedicated student to spread "Krishna Consciousness"—devotion and service to Lord Krishna— to the rest of the world.

During the next 30 years, Abhay Charan De ignored other areas of his life and devoted himself to Krishna Consciousness. In the early 1950s, his business failed, and his wife left him after selling one of his holy books to buy food. In 1954, he moved to the city of Vrindaban, India, which many people believed was the traditional home of Lord Krishna. There, he took a vow to become a wandering monk and devote his life to Krishna. Abhay adopted his new name of A. C. Bhaktivedanta Swami, and he later began using the nickname Prabhupada.

In Vrindaban, Prabhupada worked on an English translation of the Bhagavad-Gita and published a magazine entitled *Back to Godhead.* He also wrote *Easy Journey to Other Planets,* a book about Krishna Consciousness. Determined to introduce Krishna Consciousness to the English-speaking world, he left for the United States in the summer of 1965.

After arriving, Prabhupada rented a grimy studio in a poor area of New York, where he held classes on the Bhagavad-Gita for curious students, artists, and musicians.

The following year, he moved into a storefront at 26 Second Avenue, where he set up a Krishna temple. Several visitors began showing up on a daily basis to hear his lessons. Prabhupada attracted young adults who wanted to escape the problems and complications of modern life. Many of these people wanted to drop out of society permanently and become part of a close-knit, self-sufficient community.

Prabhupada told his listeners that human beings have a soul, or *atman*, that survives when the body dies and is reincarnated—reborn into a new body. The goal of Krishna worship was to get rid of ordinary wants, such as the desire for money and power, and join with this eternal soul. To achieve this, he said, a short series of phrases must be repeated to oneself or out loud. His followers chanted hundreds of verses of the *maha mantra*—the holy names of Krishna:

Hare Krishna, Hare Krishna
Krishna Krishna, Hare Hare
Hare Rama, Hare Rama
Rama Rama, Hare Hare

In September 1966, Prabhupada initiated his first American disciples and founded the International Society for Krishna Consciousness (ISKCON). Leading his followers to New York's Greenwich Village, Prabhupada helped them to perform a *sankirtan*, a public display of dancing, chanting, and devotion to Krishna. This was the first sankirtan ever seen in the United States. A small crowd watched and listened to the young "Hare Krishnas" dance and chant.

From that time on, the men and women of Krishna Consciousness spent many hours on the streets of New York, performing the sankirtan while trying to collect money for their temple on Second Avenue. Although the Krishnas believed that other religions were essentially true, they believed their religion was the most correct.

Hare Krishnas dance and chant in public to raise money for their church.

Prabhupada changed the lives of his devotees in many ways. Under his guidance, they adopted Hindu names. They altered their appearances by shaving their heads, painting clay marks on their noses and foreheads, and wearing robes like those worn by monks in India. Most Krishnas also moved into communal homes and apartments. They became vegetarians and gave up alcohol, tobacco, coffee, and tea. Every morning, they woke before sunrise and attended a religious service. During the day, they chanted the maha mantra numerous times.

By 1967, Prabhupada had attracted several hundred followers in New York City. Ready to spread his movement from Second Avenue to the rest of North America, he asked Keith Ham, a convert who had taken the name Kirtanananda, to travel to Montreal, Canada, and open a new Krishna temple. Kirtanananda eagerly carried out his assignment and won several new devotees. His success in Canada made him Prabhupada's favorite disciple.

Michael Grant, a follower who adopted the name Mukunda, went to San Francisco, where he started a Krishna temple. The area was home to thousands of young adults who had dropped out of society and were interested in Hinduism and other eastern religions. In January 1967, Mukunda asked the Grateful Dead and other bands in San Francisco to play at the Avalon Ballroom to raise money for the Hare Krishnas.

The Mantra Rock Dance was a great success, and Prabhupada appeared at the concert to give the audience

124

a lesson in Krishna chanting. Prabhupada stayed in San Francisco for five months, making converts, working on his translations, and leading his followers in public chanting in the city's Golden Gate Park.

After returning to New York, Prabhupada suffered a stroke and spent several days in the hospital. Soon after he was discharged, Prabhupada decided to return to India and take Kirtanananda with him. When they arrived in Vrindaban, Prabhupada decided to make his disciple a *sannyasi*, a monk—like Prabhupada—who has cast himself off from the rest of the world. Proud of his standing in the group, Kirtanananda prepared himself to become the new leader of the Krishna Consciousness movement.

In the summer of 1968, Prabhupada asked Kirtanananda to travel to London, England, and open a new temple there. Kirtanananda, however, had his own ideas on how to spread Krishna Consciousness. He understood Westerners better than Prabhupada and thought he had a better way to bring them into the movement. Instead of going to London, he returned to New York and explained to the Krishnas there that they should drop their newly adopted Hindu customs and rejoin mainstream society. This way, the Krishnas could gain many new members and grow into a wealthy and powerful movement.

Hearing of Kirtanananda's actions, Prabhupada wrote an angry letter to his followers in New York, criticizing his favorite disciple's ideas. Prabhupada's letter

125

split the New York temple into two hostile factions. Some Krishnas supported Kirtanananda, while others saw him as a traitor. With his support from Prabhupada gone, Kirtanananda left New York for West Virginia in 1968. There, he bought farms and fields and established a new Krishna community, which he called New Vrindaban.

Despite his problems with Kirtanananda, Prabhupada was still determined to spread Krishna Consciousness to Europe. After all, yoga (a series of exercises designed to control the body and mind), meditation (lengthy reflection on spiritual matters), reincarnation, and other Eastern ideas and practices were already popular in England, where a large community of Hindus from India had been living for many years. Late that summer, he asked Mukunda and several other followers to go to London.

After their arrival, Mukunda and the other Krishnas struck up a friendship with the Beatles, perhaps the world's most popular rock band at the time. In 1969, George Harrison, a member of the Beatles, agreed to record the Krishna chant as a three-and-a-half minute song. The "Hare Krishna Mantra" was an instant hit, selling 70,000 copies in the first day of its release. "Top of the Pops," a weekly television program that featured Britain's most popular singers and played the nation's most popular songs, invited the Krishna chanters to perform their mantra on the air. The media exposure helped

George Harrison of the Beatles, pictured here in the early 1970s, helped turn the Hare Krishnas' maha mantra *into a pop song.*

the Krishnas to bring in thousands of new recruits and establish temples throughout Europe.

Back in the United States, however, the Hare Krishna movement was changing. To maintain their temples and open new ones, Prabhupada's followers found new methods to raise money. They would chant in busy airports, hand out free books, and then ask for donations on behalf of hungry or disabled people. Although the Krishnas argued that their actions were protected by the freedom-of-religion guarantee in the U.S. Constitution, several courts ruled that the Krishnas were deceiving the public and placed limitations on their public fund-raising endeavors.

In New Vrindaban, Kirtanananda was bringing a new breed of Krishnas into his colony. Many of them were unemployed drifters, and some had criminal records. Kirtanananda's goal was not to reform his followers, but rather to raise as much money as possible. The New Vrindaban Krishnas begged for funds on the street. They also sold books and records from their vans and trucks, along with pirated T-shirts that displayed copyrighted cartoon characters. Soon, they also began selling marijuana, LSD, and other illegal drugs. Kirtanananda and his followers smuggled drugs into the United States from India and other Asian countries, and some Krishnas spent their mornings smoking dope instead of chanting.

Prabhupada knew little about the activities at New Vrindaban. But he could see that the ISKCON's rapidly growing membership was causing problems. In July 1970, he decided to reform the movement by organizing a Governing Body Commission (GBC) made up of 12 Krishna temple presidents. Prabhupada asked these leaders to renounce the everyday world and become sannyasis. Each of them would be assigned certain regions of the world as their exclusive territory. Although the individual temples would still be responsible for raising the money they needed, the GBC would set policy for the movement worldwide.

To spread Krishna Consciousness, Prabhupada also established the Bhaktivedanta Book Trust, a company that would publish Krishna literature. In addition, he planned three new temples in India—in Bombay, Mayapur, and Vrindaban—to train future leaders for the Krishna movement.

Prabhupada believed his reforms would unify the movement. But the GBC went through bitter squabbles and rivalries, as its members fought among themselves for the leadership of ISKCON. In India, Prabhupada worked hard to bring together the members of the GBC, but he was only partially successful. He traveled around the globe, hoping to solve the problems and stop the disputes among his followers. But, as his health deteriorated, Prabhupada grew more discouraged and more uncertain about building a united, worldwide faith. In 1977, he died at his home in Vrindaban.

Shortly after their leader's death, the members of the GBC announced that they, as a group, were now the divinely appointed leaders of the worldwide Krishna Consciousness movement. With unlimited power over their followers, who were bringing in vast sums of money in donations, they surrounded themselves with luxuries and lived like kings.

At this time, several Hare Krishnas took the Krishna Consciousness movement in new and very strange directions. Hans Kary (who changed his name to Hansadutta), the leader of a Krishna temple in Berkeley, California, bought a large farm in the northern part of the state. Fearing an attack by the police, as well as a worldwide nuclear war, Kary stockpiled machine guns and planned to build minefields and concrete bunkers.

Likewise, James Immel (who called himself Jayatirtha), the leader of the Krishnas in the United Kingdom, had advised his followers to take LSD. In 1982, the Governing Body Commission expelled Immel from his position. He then founded a new branch of the movement called the Peace Krishnas. This group ignored many of the rules laid down by Prabhupada for his followers. Immel took alcohol and other drugs and spent great sums of money on personal comforts. His actions

This renovated mansion in Detroit became a center for the International Society for Krishna Consciousness during the early 1980s.

led many of his devotees to turn against him. In 1987, Immel was murdered by one of his followers.

At New Vrindaban, Kirtanananda declared that he was Prabhupada's only true successor. With the money gained from fund-raising, he bought more land and raised more buildings on the property. By the early 1980s, Kirtanananda's colony at New Vrindaban covered more than 3,000 acres. Members of the colony built a dairy farm, a sawmill, a brick factory, and a school for their children.

The New Vrindaban Krishnas also built an extravagant temple, which they called the Palace of Gold. They decorated the temple with 200 tons of marble and stained-glass windows. Outside, they grew elaborate gardens and placed boats shaped like swans on a nearby lake.

Kirtanananda had also made enemies. When Steve Bryant (a follower who had taken the name Sulocana) decided to leave New Vrindaban, Kirtanananda persuaded Bryant's wife to remain in West Virginia. Vowing revenge, Bryant wrote an exposé entitled "The Guru Business," which described Kirtanananda and the leaders of the GBC as greedy and immoral. He planned to distribute the article across West Virginia.

In September 1985, the members of the GBC met to deal with Steve Bryant. They agreed to reform the organization and live more modest lives, but they also threw Bryant out of the ISKCON. Kirtanananda, who still considered himself the rightful leader of the Krishnas, ignored the GBC and their reforms.

In the next month, Michael Shockman (known as Triyogi), an ambitious New Vrindaban devotee, attacked and nearly killed Kirtanananda as he was standing near the Palace of Gold. Shockman had asked to become a sannyasi, but Kirtanannada had refused. After spending a month in the hospital, Kirtanananda returned to New Vrindaban. He bought two attack dogs to protect himself and announced that Steve Bryant, not Shockman, was responsible for the attempt on his life.

In 1986, Bryant was living on the West Coast and preparing another article, which he planned to distribute in West Virginia. By comparing the Hare Krishna movement with the suicidal Peoples Temple cult of Jonestown, Bryant hoped to convince the New Vrindaban Krishnas to abandon Kirtanananda. But shortly after Bryant arrived in West Virginia, the local police arrested him for possessing a weapon. Convinced that he was no match for the New Vrindaban colony, Bryant decided to give up his effort and return to California.

Kirtanananda had heard about Bryant's plans. Soon afterward, one of the New Vrindaban Krishnas, Thomas Drescher (called Tirtha), followed Bryant to California and on May 22, 1986, fatally shot him. Four days later, the police arrested Drescher in Ohio. Their investigation brought state police and federal agents to New Vrindaban.

On January 5, 1987, about 50 state police officers, along with agents from the FBI and the IRS, raided the colony and confiscated money, files, and Hare Krishna merchandise. In March, the GBC voted Kirtanananda out of the ISKCON, and hundreds of New Vrindaban members left the colony.

Kirtanananda accused the government of staging an attack on Hinduism and violating the U.S. Constitution's freedom-of-religion guarantee. Nevertheless, in 1990, a federal court in West Virginia indicted him for conspiring to murder Steve Bryant. He was tried and found guilty in the following year, and sentenced to a prison term of 30 years. Thomas Drescher, the murderer of Steve Bryant, was sentenced to life in prison.

During Kirtanananda's trial, the Hare Krishna movement lost many of its devotees. The inspiration that Prabhupada had provided was now gone, and his successors at New Vrindaban could not replace it from their prison cells.

Krishna Consciousness, nevertheless, has survived in several North American cities, where Krishna temples still welcome new members. The International Society for Krishna Consciousness publishes a regular magazine, the *ISKCON World Review*. At New Vrindaban, tourists still visit the Palace of Gold and take guided tours through the grounds of the Krishna colony. The maha mantra and the Bhagavad-Gita still inspire reverence for Lord Krishna and a man known as Prabhupada.

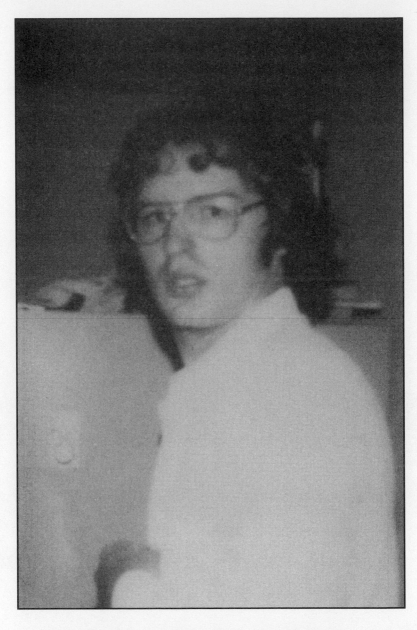

As head of the Branch Davidians, David Koresh (1959-1993) led his followers into a deadly standoff against the federal government in Waco, Texas.

8

David Koresh
The Branch Davidians

*O*n November 3, 1987, a group of eight men set out on a journey across the plains of central Texas. These men were preparing to do battle. They wore green camouflage suits and carried a stockpile of arms and ammunition in the trunks of their cars. Their destination was Mount Carmel, a hill near the town of Waco. Low sheds and ramshackle wooden houses on the hill marked the world headquarters of a small religious sect known as the Branch Davidians.

The eight men arrived at the entrance to Mount Carmel and climbed out of their cars. They removed automatic rifles and boxes of ammunition from their cars, then walked around the buildings, knocking on doors and warning the inhabitants. Vernon Wayne Howell, the leader of this group of visitors, ordered his seven followers to load their weapons and take cover.

Their target was George Roden, Howell's chief rival for control over the Branch Davidians. Roden and Howell were enemies, and Roden had suspected for some time that this showdown would take place. After hearing the intruders, Roden loaded a submachine gun and took shelter behind a tree. Soon bullets were flying across the grounds of Mount Carmel.

Despite their differences, Roden and Howell had many things in common. They had shared their faith in God and in the approaching Apocalypse—the Second Coming of Jesus Christ and the end of the world. For years, they had worked and worshiped together. But the fight would continue because both men wanted absolute control over Mount Carmel and the Branch Davidians.

The Davidians could trace their origins back to 1831, the year a Baptist preacher named William Miller concluded that the Second Coming of Christ would occur in March 1843. At that time, Miller believed, the world would be destroyed and those faithful to God would ascend to heaven.

Miller gained thousands of converts, called "Millerites," but March 1843 came and went, and the world didn't end. Another Millerite then set a second date in 1844. But when this day also passed, many Millerites abandoned their prophet in anger and disappointment.

A second group of Millerites, however, had a different conclusion. After closely studying the Bible, their leader, Ellen White, decided that God's final judgment of the faithful had already begun in heaven and that Christ's Second Coming—or Second Advent—still lay in the future. But White and her followers, who later became known as the Seventh-Day Adventists, didn't know the precise date of the end of the world.

In 1930, a Bulgarian Seventh-Day Adventist named Victor Houteff broke away from the church. Convinced that its leaders had gone astray from the teachings of Ellen White, Houteff moved to Texas, where he and about 70 followers would start a new and more pure sect of believers who would be better prepared for the Second Coming.

Houteff gathered his followers on a large tract of land near Waco, where he prepared for a gathering in the town of Palestine, about 150 miles to the east. There, Houteff planned to establish a "Kingdom of David," named after the biblical king who had used a sling to kill the Philistine giant Goliath. After proclaiming their gospel to the world, Houteff and the "Davidians" would be taken up to heaven during the Second Coming.

When Houteff died in 1955, his widow, Florence, took over the Davidians in Waco. She announced that the world would end on Easter Sunday in 1959. Hundreds of

According to the Bible, David killed the giant Goliath, then transformed the Israelites from a loosely organized group of tribes into a nation.

Seventh-Day Adventists believed her prediction and arrived in Waco that year, but Easter Sunday passed quietly. Florence Houteff, like William Miller, had been proven wrong. After this disappointment, only a few dozen Davidians remained at Waco. One of them, Benjamin Roden, established a new branch of Houteff's group, which he called the Branch Davidians. Roden died in 1978, leaving the Branch Davidians in the care of his widow, Lois.

By that time, a rowdy teenager named Vernon Wayne Howell had joined the Seventh-Day Adventist Church of Tyler, Texas. Born in 1959, Howell had dropped out of school in the ninth grade. Vernon, whose parents had never married, lived with his mother but sometimes visited his father's family. Although he was a poor student, he spent many hours reading and memorizing the family Bible, which provided him with answers to many of the questions that were troubling him. He learned to memorize long passages from both the Old and the New Testaments.

As a teenager, Vernon Howell got into trouble with other members of the local Seventh-Day Adventist congregation by standing up during services to challenge the minister and ridicule the sermon. The leaders of the church didn't appreciate Howell's disruptions, nor did they care much for his long hair, shabby clothes, and surly attitude. In 1981, they banished him from the church. Howell left Tyler and headed for Waco, where he began preaching his own sermons to the members of the Branch Davidian sect. In a loud and commanding voice, he claimed to be the seventh angel of the Book of Revelation in the Bible and the true prophet of the Second Coming.

Captivated by Howell's preaching, the Branch Davidians accepted him into their ranks. In 1983, three years before her death, Lois Roden proclaimed Howell to be her successor as the leader of the Branch Davidians. She asked the members of the sect who had left Waco to return and hear this powerful young prophet.

In 1984, Howell, then in his mid-twenties, married Rachel Jones, the 14-year-old daughter of Perry Jones, a loyal aide to Lois Roden. The marriage was Howell's way of strengthening his claim to the leadership of the sect. But George Roden, Benjamin and Lois Roden's son, believed that he—not Howell—was actually Lois Roden's rightful successor. George Roden and Vernon Howell quickly became bitter enemies. In 1985, the Branch Davidians held a leadership election and selected George Roden to be their leader. Taking over from his mother, he changed the name of Mount Carmel to Rodenville and banished Vernon Howell from the property.

Although Howell had been defeated, 40 of the Branch Davidians were still loyal to him. He took his followers to a clearing in eastern Texas, where he became the absolute leader of a small and very poor domain. Howell and his followers lived in small wooden shacks with no heat or modern plumbing. Often there was little food.

Howell gathered his followers every day for lessons and sermons. He claimed rightful ownership of all property in the camp, as well as the right to have numerous wives and mistresses. Convinced by his words—and by his amazing knowledge of the Bible—Howell's followers did not question him.

Howell traveled across much of the United States to gain new followers among members of the Seventh-Day Adventist Church. Converts from as far away as California, Hawaii, Australia, and Israel eventually heard about Howell and decided to join him in Texas. The followers were a diverse group, which included doctors, lawyers, and other professionals. Together, they prepared for the day when they would return to their rightful home in Mount Carmel.

Meanwhile, George Roden and the Branch Davidians who remained at Rodenville faced a new threat. The local courts had ruled that their compound owed more than $60,000 in property taxes. By 1987, the authorities were threatening to condemn and sell the property if Roden did not pay the taxes. But Roden had only a few followers remaining and very little money.

Desperate to hold onto his property, Roden planned a miracle. He would revive the dead body of Anna Hughes, a Branch Davidian who was buried near the compound. This would bring him thousands of new followers and, with their help, would save Rodenville from Vernon Howell. With several helpers, he dug up the casket containing the remains of Anna Hughes and moved it to the Branch Davidian chapel.

Upon hearing of Roden's actions, Vernon Howell and his followers created a plan of their own. They would gather their guns and ammunition, then enter the Waco compound to take photographs of the corpse of Anna

Hughes. They would use the pictures to discredit George Roden and show he was a "false prophet." On the morning of November 3, they set out from Palestine for Waco. There, Roden and Howell and his seven followers tried to settle their differences with bullets.

The local police arrived 45 minutes later, and Vernon Wayne Howell and George Roden put down their weapons. Roden, who had suffered a slight flesh wound, had been the only one injured in the fight. The police spread out across Mount Carmel and confiscated weapons. They arrested Howell and his accomplices, then drove them to the town jail.

Howell was charged with attempted murder, but his seven followers managed to raise enough money to bail him out of jail and pay the back taxes owed on the Waco property. George Roden, meanwhile, angered local police departments and judges by filing lawsuits and accusing the authorities of conspiring against him. Judge Walter Smith ordered Roden to "cease and desist" his legal maneuvers. In March 1988, after Roden filed more papers, the county court jailed him for contempt.

Howell's trial took place in April 1988. In court, he testified that he had driven to Waco to rebury the body of Anna Hughes. Both Howell and Roden claimed that the other man had been the first to open fire during the shootout. Unlike Howell, who remained calm and articulate on the stand, Roden seemed unstable and often used profanity. Howell's jury split on its verdict—nine jurors thought he was guilty, three thought he was not guilty—and the court declared a mistrial. Eventually, the state of Texas dropped all charges against Howell.

With their tax payment giving them a legal claim to the property, Howell and his followers in Palestine, Texas, returned to the Waco property. On May 4, they reburied Anna Hughes in the Branch Davidian cemetery. Abandoned by the Branch Davidians, Roden eventually moved to Odessa, Texas. In 1989, he murdered a 56-year-old man and was sentenced to a state mental hospital.

With George Roden locked away, Howell became the undisputed leader of the Branch Davidians. He saw himself as similar to the biblical King David, the legendary ruler of the ancient Israelites. He also preached that Armageddon—the final battle between good and evil that was prophesied in the Bible—would occur in Texas, and soon.

In the summer of 1990, Howell changed his name to David Koresh. David stood for King David of the Bible, while Koresh was the Hebrew name for Cyrus, an ancient Persian ruler. David Koresh—formerly Vernon Howell—was now the king of Mount Carmel.

To prepare for Armageddon, the Davidians tore down the old buildings on the compound and turned Mount Carmel into a heavily armed camp. They raised a wall of long, low buildings topped by a three-story watchtower, with windows facing in all directions. The

Davidians dug underground tunnels in case of an aerial attack, and they built a shooting range for target practice.

Koresh convinced his followers that his word was divine law. The families now living at the compound gave up their money and belongings. Married couples allowed Koresh to break up their families. Men, women, and children slept in separate dormitories. Koresh also illegally married himself to several women who were already married, claiming that their former husbands would eventually find their perfect mates in heaven after their deaths. Koresh fathered many children and announced that he would someday rule the world.

Not all of Koresh's followers liked his plans, however. Marc Breault, a Branch Davidian from Australia, left the compound when Koresh tried to marry Breault's wife, Elizabeth. The Breaults returned to Australia, where they spoke publicly about the troubles they had witnessed in Waco.

Marc Breault won several more Australian Davidians over to his side. In September 1990, they hired a private detective named Geoffrey Hassock to carry their statements about Koresh to the district attorney and the sheriff of McLennan County, whose jurisdiction included Mount Carmel. Hassock delivered the complaints, but the authorities told him they needed more evidence before they could act.

Koresh heard about the complaints that the Breaults were filing against him. Fearing an attack from the outside world, he increased security at the compound and told his followers to prepare for war. Armed guards patrolled the compound and nearby roads, while Koresh directed military drills and maneuvers from within the compound. Convinced that he and his followers would soon die in a final battle, he began to call the compound Ranch Apocalypse.

In early 1992, the sound of gunfire at Ranch Apocalypse began to draw complaints from people living near the compound. In May, a delivery driver told the local sheriff that a package for the Branch Davidians had accidentally broken open—and the package contained hand grenades, which are illegal for private citizens to have. The McLennan County sheriff's office reported this incident to the U.S. Bureau of Alcohol, Tobacco, and Firearms (ATF).

The ATF agents traced more than 8,000 pounds of ammunition and weapons to the Branch Davidians, including M-16 rifles, grenade launchers, and other military supplies that were illegal to own. ATF officials decided to rent a house near Ranch Apocalypse and post undercover agents there to watch Koresh. An ATF undercover agent named Robert Rodriguez joined the cult to monitor Koresh's activities.

In the autumn and winter of 1992, the agency began to draw up plans for a raid on the compound. Although ATF agents knew that Koresh spent much of his time in local restaurants, bars, and shops, they decided to make a surprise assault on the compound rather than arrest the Davidian leader when he was alone and unprotected.

Although plans for the assault were secret, the Branch Davidians and most of the other people in Waco knew that ATF agents were in town. Agents were staying in local motels and walking down the streets in their distinctive uniforms. Reporters from the Waco *Tribune-Herald* also learned of a planned operation directly from ATF agents.

On February 27, 1993, the *Tribune-Herald* newspaper ran an article entitled "Sinful Messiah," which described Koresh's stockpile of weapons, his preparations for battle, and reports that he had abused children living in the compound. ATF officials worried that this article would ignite a massive public outcry demanding that action be taken against the sect. Because of this, the agency decided to proceed with the raid immediately. On the morning of February 28, more than 100 heavily armed agents boarded three camouflaged cattle trucks and headed for Ranch Apocalypse.

By the time the agents reached the compound, a Davidian living in Waco had already told Koresh about the impending raid. Robert Rodriguez, who had escaped early that morning from Ranch Apocalypse, warned ATF officials that the Branch Davidians were waiting for them.

Behind the walls and windows of the compound, Koresh and his followers prepared for the raid. As the first group of ATF officers leapt from their trucks and

Agents from the Bureau of Alcohol, Tobacco, and Firearms stand at their base of operations near Ranch Apocalypse in Waco, Texas. The signs behind them point to the hometowns of the ATF officers involved in the operation.

reached the compound's entrance, bullets began flying from inside the compound. The ATF agents scrambled to find cover on the plains surrounding Ranch Apocalypse.

The firefight continued for two hours. At noon, the two groups called a truce. Four ATF agents died in the attack, and several agents were wounded. Inside the compound, several Branch Davidians had also lost their lives. By afternoon, television and newspaper reporters from around the nation were arriving in Waco to cover the story.

The ATF told Koresh that he could surrender and come out safely, but Koresh refused. He claimed that he had been wounded and that one of his daughters had been killed. Koresh promised to release followers who wished to leave Ranch Apocalypse on the condition that he could broadcast his messages on a local radio station.

Koresh and nearly 100 of his followers remained inside the compound. Koresh knew he would be jailed if he surrendered. The ATF did not want to risk more deaths by storming the compound again, so the standoff continued into March, when the FBI moved in to assist the ATF.

The government agencies used many different methods to try to force Koresh and his followers to

On March 9, 1993, two weeks after federal agents first attacked, a sign hangs from a window at Ranch Apocalypse, saying, "God help us. We want the press."

surrender. They allowed no food or other supplies into the compound. To keep the Branch Davidians from sleeping, the agents shone bright lights into the compound at night. Loudspeakers played music, chanting, and a tape recording of screaming rabbits.

The FBI gradually lost patience and decided to stop allowing people out of Ranch Apocalypse. By doing that, the agents hoped to increase pressure on Koresh to surrender or else to start a rebellion among his followers. On March 24, the last Branch Davidian wishing to get out of the compound did so, leaving about 90 of David Koresh's followers inside.

In early April, Koresh announced that he had received a message directly from God commanding him to write an interpretation of the seven seals of the Book of Revelation, which many biblical scholars believe describes the end of the world. As soon as Koresh was finished writing, he said, he would release the interpretation publicly and then give himself up to the authorities. But as the days dragged on and nothing happened, the leaders of the FBI concluded that Koresh was stalling. Because of the nationwide media attention given to Koresh and the government's failure to end the standoff, officials in the FBI and the Department of Justice decided to force the Branch Davidians out of the compound with tear gas.

Early on the morning of April 19, the FBI attacked the compound with cranes to knock holes in the compound buildings and heavy tanks to shoot dozens of

149

This vendor sold merchandise during the highly publicized 1993 showdown between the federal government and the Branch Davidians in Waco, Texas.

tear gas canisters inside. It is questionable what exactly was happening inside the compound as the flammable tear gas spread. Around noon, the compound caught on fire. A dry wind was blowing, and within minutes the buildings were in flames. After 51 days, the standoff had ended. The cause of the fire remains the subject of intense scrutiny to this day.

The FBI and the members of the press watched as 78 Branch Davidians died a terrible, painful death. Koresh himself, along with several other members of the cult, died of gunshot wounds while the buildings burned around them. Eleven people escaped the fire, but 17 children, many of them Koresh's own, died in a second-story room.

The fire caused an outcry among religious organizations, which claimed the Branch Davidians were victims of an illegal assault by the government. Attorney General Janet Reno, the head of the Department of Justice, testified on the case before the U.S. Congress and claimed full responsibility for the April attack on the compound.

By the end of 1993, the federal government brought the Branch Davidians who had survived the fire to trial for conspiracy and for killing four of the federal agents who raided the compound. The defendants, all facing up to

Janet Reno, who publicly assumed responsibility for the 1993 attack on the Branch Davidians, had become the U.S. attorney general only a few weeks before the conflict began.

life sentences in prison, claimed they had acted in self-defense. In February 1994, nearly one year after the raid had begun, the 11 Branch Davidians were found not guilty of murder. But in June 1994, eight of them were found guilty of possessing illegal weapons and received prison sentences ranging from 5 to 40 years.

Although few people sympathized with David Koresh or his followers, many people believed the government still had no cause to mount such a large and heavily-armed raid on a small, isolated religious group.

Branch Davidian members Kevin Whitecliff (left), Brad Branch (middle), and Livingstone Fagan (right) are taken into custody.

Bibliography

Atack, John. *A Piece of Blue Sky: Scientology, Dianetics, and L. Ron Hubbard Exposed.* New York: Carol Publishing Group, 1990.

Bailey, Brad. *Mad Man in Waco.* Waco, TX: WRS Publishing, 1993.

Barker, Eileen. *The Making of a Moonie.* Oxford, England: Basil Blackwell, 1984.

Bushman, Richard L. *Joseph Smith and the Beginnings of Mormonism.* Urbana: University of Illinois Press, 1984.

Goswami, Satsvarupa Dasa. *Prabhupada.* Los Angeles: The Bhaktivedanta Book Trust, 1983.

Hubner, John, and Lindsey Gruson. *Monkey on a Stick: Murder, Madness, and the Hare Krishnas.* New York: Harcourt Brace Jovanovich, 1988.

Kautsky, Karl. *Communism in Central Europe in the Time of the Reformation.* New York: Augustus M. Kelley, 1966.

Kilduff, Marshall. *Suicide Cult: The Inside Story of the Peoples Temple Sect and the Massacre in Guyana.* New York: Bantam, 1978.

Klineman, George. *The Cult that Died: The Tragedy of Jim Jones and the Peoples Temple.* New York: Putnam, 1980.

Krause, Charles A. *Guyana Massacre: The Eyewitness Account.* New York: Berkeley Publishing, 1978.

Madigan, Tim. *See No Evil: Blind Devotion and Bloodshed in David Koresh's Holy War.* Fort Worth, TX: The Summit Group, 1993.

Miller, Russell. *Bare Faced Messiah: The True Story of L. Ron Hubbard.* New York: Holt, 1988.

Reston, James. *Our Father Who Art in Hell.* New York: Times Books, 1981.

Sontag, Frederick. *Sun Myung Moon and the Unification Church.* Nashville: Abingdon Press, 1977.

Watts, Jill. *God, Harlem, U.S.A.: The Father Divine Story.* Berkeley: University of California Press, 1992.

Yamamoto, J. Isamu. *The Puppet Master: An Inquiry into Sun Myung Moon and the Unification Church.* Downers Grove, IL: InterVarsity Press, 1977.

Index

cults, definition, 8-9

David (biblical figure), 137, 138, 143
Dianetic Research Foundation, 69, 70, 71
Dianetics: The Modern Science of Mental Health, 68, 69
Divine, Father, 44, 45-46, 51, 102, 107; businesses of, 54-55, 58; death of, 63; followers of, 51-52, 53, 54; 59, 61; Kingdom of, 52, 53; Peace Missions of, 53, 54-56, 58, 59, 60-61, 62-63, 102; political platform of, 55-56; scandals involving, 56-57, 58-61; trial of, 52-53, *See also* Baker, George, Jr.; and Messenger, the
Divine, Mother, 51, 61, 63
Divine Principle, The, 86, 87, 88
Doniphan, Alexander, 35
Drescher, Thomas (Tirtha), 132, 133
Dunklin, Daniel, 33

Faithful Mary, 54, 58-59
faith healing, 8, 100, 101, 106
Father Divine, *See* Divine, Father
Federal Bureau of Investigation, 57, 62, 77, 105, 133; and raid on Branch Davidians, 148-151
Ford, Thomas, 39, 40-41

God, 18, 29, 31, 40, 44, 48, 50, 51, 56, 57, 58, 84, 86, 87, 101, 136, 137, 148, 149
gods, 7, 120
Goswami, Bhaktisiddhanta Sarasvati, 121
Governing Body Commission (GBC), 128, 129, 130, 131-132, 133
Grant, Michael (Mukunda), 124, 126
Guardian's Office, 75, 78

Ham, Keith (Kirtanananda), 124, 125-126, 128, 131-133
Han, Hak Ja, 93, 97
Hansadutta (Hans Kary), 129-130
Hare Krishnas, 6, 123-124, 127, 129, 132, 133, *See also* Krishna Consciousness movement
Harris, Don, 114
Harris, Martin, 27, 34
Harrison, George, 126, 127
Hassock, Geoffrey, 144
heaven, 12, 26, 49, 84, 136, 137, 144
hinduism, 120, 124, 125, 126, 133
Hitchings, Edna Rose, 61-62
Holy Communion banquets, 45-46, 49, 50, 51, 53
Holy Spirit, 48, 87
Houteff, Florence, 137-138
Houteff, Victor, 137
Howell, Vernon Wayne, 136, 139; early years of, 139; followers of, 140-141; as leader of Branch Davidians, 139-141; name change, 143; struggle with George Roden, 135-136, 140-142; trial of, 142-143, *See also*, Koresh, David
Hubbard, Harry, 66
Hubbard, L. Ron (La Fayette Ronald): accusations against, 64, 70-71, 73-75, 78; as businessman, 69-70, 73, 74; and Church of Scientology, 65, 71-77, 81; death of, 79; early years of, 66; fortune of,

158

ABOUT THE AUTHOR

TOM STREISSGUTH, born in Washington, D.C., in 1958, graduated from Yale University, where he studied history, literature, languages, and music. He has traveled widely in Europe and the Middle East, and has worked as a teacher, editor, and journalist. Streissguth is also the author of *Communications: Sending the Message, Hatemongers and Demagogues, Hoaxers and Hustlers, International Terrorists, Legendary Labor Leaders, Soviet Leaders from Lenin to Gorbachev,* and *Utopian Visionaries.* He lives in Sarasota, Florida, with his wife and two daughters.

Photo Credits

Photographs courtesy of The Bettmann Archive: pp. 6, 50, 54, 59, 64, 77, 80 (both), 82, 93, 96, 98, 109, 111, 113, 117, 118, 123, 127, 130, 138, 148, 152; Bundesarchiv, Germany, pp. 10, 14, 18; Library of Congress, pp. 13, 22, 24, 28, 30, 36, 37, 57, 84, 91, 103; Missouri State Archives, p. 43; Minnesota Historical Society, pp. 44, 60; Maryland Historical Society, Baltimore, p. 47; MacArthur Memorial, p. 86; Indiana Historical Society, p. 101; Wide World Photos, Inc., p. 134; Texas State Library, Archives Division, pp. 147, 150; and U.S. Department of Justice, p. 151.